EBENEZER

A Brief Memoir of a Long Life Full of Merciful Incidents

By Richard Breeze, Swindon

edited and annotated by Julia Revak

Calgary, Alberta, 2008

Order this book online at www.trafford.com

or email orders@trafford.com

Most Trafford titles are also available at major online book retailers.

Printed in Victoria, BC, Canada.

ISBN: 978-1-4251-6434-8

*Our mission is to efficiently provide the world's finest, most comprehensive
book publishing service, enabling every author to experience success.
To find out how to publish your book, your way, and have it available
worldwide, visit us online at www.trafford.com/10510*

Trafford rev. 3/2/2009

 www.trafford.com

North America & international
toll-free: 1 888 232 4444 (USA & Canada)
phone: 250 383 6864 ♦ fax: 812 355 4082

PREFACE

IN 1975, MY parents returned to England for a holiday, and to visit family. In the "junk room" in the old Breeze family home, my father came across the hand-written memoir of the Rev. Richard Breeze. He had heard very little about his great-grandfather, and was intrigued by the memoir. His brother was not interested in the Breeze family history at the time, and suggested he take it with him.

My father and mother spent a week in Wales visiting some of the villages where Richard Breeze had grown up, and even managed to identify some of Richard Breeze's family homes around Llanwnog, Llandinam and Llanbrynmair.

Richard and his wife Sarah, as he mentions in Chapter 15, A Few Tales of Cruel Deeds, lost three of their six children. His eldest son, William Beckingsale, died at twenty one, one daughter, Sarah Susannah, died at fourteen, and Samuel Pearce, twin to Elizabeth Beckingsale Breeze, died at eleven weeks of age. The Rev. Richard Breeze retired in 1865, though not completely, and died in 1878 at Eastbourne, Sussex, aged eighty. His widow, Sarah, died at eighty two, in 1887 at Hastings, Sussex.

His surviving son, Richard Goodwin Breeze, became a doctor, and died at age forty seven, leaving his widow, Martha, to raise and educate their nine surviving children.

Richard Breeze's eldest surviving daughter, Elizabeth Beckingsale Breeze, was running her own school by 1881, and died in 1889. Mary Breeze, his youngest daughter, died in 1906. By that year, she was living with her sister-in-law Martha Breeze, and, was probably responsible for the survival of the Breeze papers.

Some years later, I transcribed Richard Breeze's memoir for my father, who had become ill. As I read his memoir, I developed an admiration for Richard Breeze's achievements, and have attempted to publish it as he would have wished.

Julia Revak

CONTENTS

EBENEZER | *Richard Breeze, Swindon*

1

BIRTH AND PARENTAGE

MY WORTHY PARENTS, William and Susannah Breeze, at the time of my birth occupied a small farm, called Pound farm, in the parish of Llanwonog, in the county of Montgomery, North Wales. My father was a worthy man; honest, upright, and truly noble in all his actions–rather stern, but much respected and even beloved, by all who knew him best.

My mother was a model of good temper and gentleness; sweet, lovely, and very much beloved. I do not recollect ever seeing her in a passion. Dear woman, I love to think about her, and muse upon her memory. Peace be to her ashes. We shall meet again.

Though my beloved parents possessed many great excellencies, still they were, I fear, at this time, and for many years afterwards, strangers to Jesus Christ, and to the way of salvation through him.

I was born on the first Tuesday in the month of August 1797[1], and baptized at the Parish Church, on the third of September, being the month following, 1797, according to a certificate received from the Clergyman of the Parish, which is as follows:

"Richard, Son of William and Susannah Breeze, his wife, was baptized the 3rd of Sep. 1797–This is to certify that the above is a copy of the entry in the Register Book of Baptisms of the Church of Llanwonog, and the county of Montgomery. "Witness my hand this 10th of Sep. 1833.

David James, Curate, Llanwonog aforesaid".

---

[1] The first Tuesday in August, 1797, was the 1st of August of that year.

My beloved parents had eight children; four sons, and four daughters.[2] I was the third son. Soon after my birth, England was visited with a partial famine. Wheat was sold at the high price of 20sh or 30sh per bushel; at which time my father did much in the mealing business, which answered his purpose very well, and enabled him to help many a starving family; by giving much away to some, and granting long credit to others, who were honest and likely to pay. I have heard my parents say that this was to them a prosperous year, God blessing them in return for their sympathy for the poor and needy in this their time of trouble.

Pound farm, where I drew my first breath, may appear to the eye of a stranger as not at all likely to confer honour upon any one born in that humble locality; and may well elicit the question, can any good thing come out of this place? As I have not the vanity to think that I can confer any honour upon the place of my nativity myself, I must look for it elsewhere. If ancient records are true, I believe I can establish the fact that I am truly a citizen of no mean city; and that if I may fail to impart dignity to the place of my birth, as many have done, I hope I can make it sufficiently clear that the place of my birth may invest me with honours of no common order.

That which is to me a sacred spot is situated in the rich and lovely Vale of the Severn within about one mile of its clear, bright, and sparkling streams. It lies within one mile and a half of an ancient Roman city, once of great celebrity, but now only a hamlet, or village, called Cairsws, but which in former times extended for several miles along the banks of the Severn even to the place of my birth, as there are streets and lanes, and some remains of hollow-arched fosses, &c, &c, to be seen even to the present day.

---

[2] William Brees/Breeze, Susannah Goodwin and their children: William Breeze, b. *ca* 1758, estimate based on age at death, in Llanbrynmair, Montgomeryshire, at Coidlynain Farm. Married, 22 December 1781, Wm. Brees, Carno, Br. and Susannah Goodwin, dau of Edward Goodwin and __ Hughes, of Llandinam. Susanna Brees, Clogau, bur 17 May 1823, aged 65. William Brees, Clogau, bur. 23 May 1829.

Children of William and Susannah Breeze: Susanneh, bap. 3? May 1782; Ursula, bap. 9 May 1784; William, bap. 27 May 1787; Jane, bap. 14 March 1790; Annamariah, bap. 17 June 1792; Edward, bap. 10 Aug. 1793; Richard; Fourth son not found in Llanwonog records. [Records of children's baptisms from film of Bishop's Transcripts, Llanwonog, Montgomery. Read at Family History Centre, Calgary]

There are the forms of three camps still to be seen in the locality, making nearly a triangle, which were most likely for the defence of the city. The one was Gwyn Vynydd, some 200 yards from our house. The second was called Rhos Ddiarbed, and the third in the parish of Llandinam, of a very uncommon form, having at the south end a large conic mount, surrounded by a deep fosse. Some sixty years ago some bricks and mortar were dug up out of this camp, which were afterwards used in building a chimney of a neighbouring public house. One brick had the following in *alto-relievo,* "*CICIPB*", which some here read *Caius Iulius Cesar, Imperator*. There was formerly a Castle in this city, but its extent is now unknown. The Roman road, called *Sarn Swsan* runs here, pointing to Meifod, and may be clearly traced to the banks of the Tyrowy near to Slysin. The strong men with hard hands, with spades and mattocks, do every now and then turn up portions of it in every part in the line it takes.

Roman coins are occasionally picked up in this locality. One interesting circumstance came under my own observation about 45 years ago. A good man whom I well knew, of the name of Williams, working on his employer's farm, while in the act of digging a hole for a gate post, and wishing in his heart that he had money to give in the morrow at the opening of the new Baptist Chapel at Cairsws, picked up a piece of coin out of the dirt, I believe a Roman gold piece. He was advised to go to Mr. Jones, silversmith, of Newtown. He went, and received 10sh for it, which he put on the plate on the morrow, with heartfelt delight. What a lesson! He wished he had the power to give, and God gave him that power and he used it.

It is true that this neighbourhood is not what it once was. The architectural glory, its crowded streets, and military evolutions, are now no more; all is quiet and silent. Still, you may in a measure, bring up the past, and in your imagination revel luxuriously among the former glories of the place.

You fancy you see this magnificent Roman city stretched before you in this lovely Vale, covering many acres of land. On the left stands the noble castle in all its strength and majesty, and a little more distant in the same direction you see the fort, or grand entrance into the city from the East, since called the Porth, where there is now a junction of the Newtown and Aberystwyth Railway. Right ahead, on that high hill, in the parish of

Llandinam, you see the large camp once alive with soldiers, as if preparing for a vigorous defence. Then somewhat more to the right you behold another camp filled with soldiers on the look out, as if they expected an enemy advancing toward the city. What about the camp close by? a few paces from the dear spot of earth, the place of my birth? There, I find, throngs are all on the move, a scene of activity and bustle is witnessed all through the camp, and about it on every side. Being near the men, I could very distinctly see their persons, and truly they were a fine race of men. There they stood, bold and valiant to a man, fearless of danger, fine, Roman cohorts, who had stood firmly through many a tough campaign. Always triumphant. They never gave their back to the foe. The officers, fine and gentlemanly. The trumpet was blown to summon the warriors together, and one of them addressed them eloquently and sufficiently aloud, so that I could hear a few words, and was able to make out something that was said, though not distinctly.

He said that it was a false alarm and thanked them for their readiness for action, for their cool and determined bravery. "It well became their position, as they were then in an enemy's country, one mistake might be death to them all, and such an enemy," said he, with much warmth, and an elevated voice, "nowhere else is to be found."

"My brave men, I will not conceal from you the fact that these Britons are true heroes. They fight like lions. Nothing but Roman bravery and superior numbers can possibly stand before them. My brave soldiers," continued he, "as today, be ever ready, as the next report of the kind may be true. I may as well inform you, as I never wish to keep any secret from my brave men, that it was reported yesterday that Llewellin ap Jor with ap Rhys, that great Warrior and truly great hero of North Wales was rapidly advancing at the head of a large army to give us battle. But why he altered his plans, I am not able to inform you."

Another officer, of a mild and gentle countenance next addressed the men, "Warriors and fellow-soldiers, we all feel thankful to our noble General for his address, and for the good advice it contained. He said he could not inform you why the great King of the North altered his plans, and did not come to give us battle. If I give my own opinion I feel assured that the noble-minded General will not be offended at what I am going to say. Now some of you in these heroic ranks are Christians. We believe in Christ Jesus. We believe in the true God. It was he who turned the heart of the British hero for some hidden purpose, known only to himself. It may be to give us a merciful respite, and, by and by, to bring about peace and friendship between us and so brave a foe."

He said more to the same effect, but less distinctly. Still I could catch a few broken sentences about the all-powerful foe, and the desirableness of peace and goodwill between them, and that those present who loved Jesus Christ, ought, above all others, to pray earnestly and without ceasing to God to bring soon to pass the Angels' song at the birth of the Dear Redeemer, "Glory to God in the highest, on earth peace, and goodwill toward men."

I need not say that sentiments like these, coming from such a quarter, filled my heart with joy, and my mind with confidence. I ventured to stroll nearer to them, keeping my eye upon the last speaker, for he had not only excited my curiosity, but mightily warmed my heart towards him.

I at length caught his eye and respectfully approached him, and smilingly said,

"Sir, I am delighted to hear you give expression to such sublime sentiments."

"Sir," said he, with a countenance radiant with smiles, "and I am exceedingly glad to hear you make use of such good words, as it leads me to hope that you also love the Dear Redeemer."

While engaged in interesting and profitable conversation I found myself soon surrounded by a large group of men, officers and common soldiers, with faces beaming with delight; each man wishing to speak first upon the great Salvation. It was a Babel, a Babel of Christian love.

"Sir, are you a Christian," asks one.

"Have you ever been to Rome?" asks another.

"Dear Sir," asks a third, "have you ever heard the Venerable Paul, the aged, preach the glorious gospel?"

Then several spoke out at the same time.

"Sir, have you ever seen the lovely and ever to be beloved Claudia, the

British princess?"

Well, well, thought I, this is overwhelming, and I anxiously looked out for a way of escape. It was really too much for my physical and mental powers to bear. I retreated, blundering out an apology in the best way I could, saying, "Will call again at an early day."

I did call again and again. Refreshing, truly, were those delightful visits to the Roman camp. I found that the Christianity of these men was of an uncommon order. It was indeed of the most exalted kind I ever witnesses. Why was it? Why! They had drunk of the waters of truth at the fountain-head, before it had been polluted by the feet of the wicked Beast. Before Antichrist was born. Before truth became mixed with error. Their views of Divine truth as clear as the Scriptures itself, the only source from which they fetched them. Baptists to a man—no Ritualists—no Popery men—not they.

I shall never forget their smile of approbation, when I told them that I had followed the Lord through the waters of baptism, and had met with the Lord's people at this table to commemorate the dying love of the dear Redeemer. But! I must close my happy musings, loath as I am to part with them. It is tearing myself away from the best society.

In awaking from my pleasant reverie I ask myself if this happy dream were true. To this I reply that history fails us, but that there was once in this locality a great city, a Roman city, there can be no mistake. We have the ruins of ancient grandeur before our eyes, and all the vestiges of antiquity already named; the ruins of the old Castle, the Fort, the three Roman camps, the Roman road, the fosses, the arches, and numerous coins, &c.

Who can object to my sweet musings and say they are not inspirations? We know that there were many Christians among the Roman legions. Who is bold enough to say that Cornelius, Captain of the Italian band, of whom the disciples said to their Divine Master, "He loveth our nation, and hath built us a synagogue," was never here? Who can say he never graced the place of my birth with his presence, marching over the spot at the head of his faithful band of soldiers?

But a truce to questionings. Look at the locality with the eyes and the feelings of a Christian philosopher. Look at the ground just here. How many thousands, yes, hundreds of thousands of human beings, it may be, lie interred in this lovely Vale? They shall all arise to life again. How many of them will have a joyful resurrection? Lord, so teach us to number our days, that we may apply our hearts unto wisdom.

I close this chapter with the beautiful lines of Bishop Heber, making a trifling alteration to suit our position as dwellers in this beautiful land of the free and the brave, this pearl of the ocean so bright.

> What though refreshing breezes
> Blow soft o'er Britain's Isles;
> Though every prospect pleases,
> And only man is vile;
> Ye saints wish lavish kindness
> The gifts of God are strewen.
> The heathen in his blindness
> Bows down to wood and stones.
>
> Waft, waft, ye winds his story,
> And you, ye waters roll.
> Till, like a sea of glory,
> It spreads from pole to pole;
> Till o'er our ransomed nation
> The Lamb for sinners slain.
> Redeemer, King, Creator
> In bliss returns to reign.

2

REMOVAL TO ANOTHER FARM. KEYBREN

THIS WAS, UPON the whole, a very pleasant change. The farm was somewhat larger, and, perhaps, superior in quality. Bounded on the north and the east by the Cairginog estate, the extensive property of C.H. Tracey Esq., Cairginog Hall[1] is a fine residence, and beautifully situated. I used to think, when a boy, that good King George the third had not a house to live in much larger than this, and was not a much greater man than the worthy Esquire at the Hall, a kind gentleman, a good landlord, and a very condescending and just master to the numerous labourers he employed on his estates. I well remember that these men, their wives and their children almost adored the worthy gentleman. So the name of Tracey has sounded pleasant in my ears for more than sixty years. One circumstance, though in itself trivial, still lingers in my memory. It is said that the Squire had much wit and humour. One day he saw a sturdy beggar approach.

---

[1] Now Gregynog Hall, the house is about a hundred and fifty years old, though parts of an older house have been incorporated, and there has been a hall on the site since at least the 12th century. From the 15th century onwards Gregynog was the seat of the Blayney family (Blaenau in Welsh) until Arthur Blayney died in 1795, a bachelor. There are many references to it in the poetry of the period, it seems to have been particularly noteworthy for its hospitality. In the 19th century the house belonged to the Hanbury Tracys, later the Sudeleys. In the 1840s Henry Hanbury Tracy pulled the old house down and rebuilt it in its present form, later adding the fake concrete 'half-timbering'. He was a pioneer in the use of concrete as a building material.(He built the concrete cottages, farmhouses and the school in Tregynon.) The Sudeleys lost money in the Newtown flannel industry and in 1894 sold the Gregynog estate to Lord Joicey who kept it until 1914, when the estate (18,000 acres) was broken up and sold, mainly to tenants of the farms and cottages. [From: *University Conference Centre - History and tradition* website / University of Wales at: http://www.wales.ac.uk/defaultpage.asp?page=E3003]

He met him and said, "My man, go up to the front door and knock with all your strength, then the ladies will hear you." He, at the meantime, placed himself behind a bush in the shrubbery to enjoy the fun of it. The fellow knocked lustily. The servants rushed to the door as if they feared the house was falling, and then the ladies came and, on seeing the beggar, were loud in their threats of the Constable &c. The beggar stood there confused and frightened, and was glad to start off empty-handed, so as to escape the storm. The gentleman enjoyed his humour, and meeting the terrified fugitive put half a crown into his hand, saying, "fear not." Very likely the gentleman went indoors next to pacify the ladies by explaining the matter, and to enjoy a good family laugh over it.

Our farm was bounded on the south and the west by a farm, the property of a young man who was afterward married to my eldest sister.

He sold a portion of his lower field for building purposes, so that a number of houses were built on the various sites. An Independent Chapel was also erected in the place, which soon became a centre of attraction for several miles around, and doubtless, hundreds of precious souls have been gathered to Jesus Christ through this circumstance.

The name given to this newly created village is Bwlch-y-frith, or nich, or gullet: i.e. an opening between two hills for water to pass. If it had not been for this Bwlch the water would cover the frith, or pastures above, and, most likely, form an inland lake of considerable size. It reminds us of Clifton. God did there, as here, by some mighty operation on nature, cleave asunder these rocks for the passing away of the waters for the benefit of man. How unsearchable is his wisdom, and his ways past finding out.

The state of morals was, when we first went to this neighbourhood, awfully bad. The Sabbaths were fearfully desecrated, and no moral influence exerted, that I know of, to prevent that sad state of things. There was no Chapel then, and the parish Church was about four miles off. The roads to get there were so awfully bad, so many rough gates with clumsy latches to open, that it was truly a formidable affair to go to the church, the mill or the market, or anywhere else.

Many thanks to C.R.Tracey Esq. of the present day. A gentleman, from what I can learn, truly worthy of his great ancestor who ruled so well in the early part of this century. This gentleman has recently made a good road from his noble residence, through Bwlch-y-frith to Glanrhyd, and onward to the highroad to Newtown, passing by the parish Church. I should say the good people in the various localities are very thankful to him for this great improvement. At least, they ought to be, and I have no doubt they are.

The moral condition of the people was actually worse than the bad roads, and all other physical evils put together. The meadows below our house were for some time a place of resort for the Sabbath breakers. Here all manner of rural sports were carried on; football, bandy, Cat, &c. &c., and that in the presence of the Churchwarden himself, and in his own fields, for my father had been appointed to this office on his coming to reside in this parish.

Why did he, as a parish officer especially, allow of such doings? Why indeed? The only apology I have to offer for my kind father, and for many others in the locality, is the universal practice of the age. Even Clergymen of the Church have patronized these games on God's holy day, yes, and more, these ungodly sports have been framed by law, and patronized by men in authority. Witness the book of sports. Thanks be to God for better days. May they still improve.

A merciful change came over this neighbourhood at length. A new Independent Chapel was opened at Bwlch-y-frith. Several persons, far and near, who had wept and sighed for years over the sad state of things, came forward to assist the new undertaking. The Chapel was well supplied with good Ministers. A Sunday School was opened. Week evening services were held. Singing meetings and other services for the benefit of the young commenced. Oh, it was delightful! The fields became deserted, the sports were given up, the loud noises over the games and the bad words too often used, were exchanged for prayer and praise.

Why, the fields, the lanes, the woods and the dells echoed loudly and sweetly to the songs of Zion. The good practice continues to this day, and may it continue to the end of time.

Soon afterwards a Commercial Day School was opened in a part of the Chapel, and was conducted by Mr. Thomas Roberts, Brother to the Rev^d

John Roberts of Llanbrynmair. This was found to be very convenient, and a good number of young people came to receive its advantages.

Here I also received the first elements of my education. Among the rest, one came to improve himself in the English language, preparatory to his entering the Congregational College at Wrexham. This was Mr. William Williams, a young gentleman, so good, so devout, and so loving, that to see him was to love him. He was kind, and so tender to us all that he soon gained the warmest affection of every boy in the School. He would often take us little ones on his knee, and talk to us so nicely about Jesus Christ, about heaven, and about everything else that was at all likely to lead our youthful minds to sacred and divine things. Once he lovingly put his hand upon my head, saying, with such a sweet smile, "Ah! this dear little boy may become a minister of the gospel." That seemed almost prophetic, although I thought at the time that no such honour would ever fall to my lot. He could not preach in the English language, to the great regret of those of us who did not understand the Welsh. However it was reported one day that he was going to preach at the Chapel. We waited with much impatience for the time. It came at last. The text he had chosen for the occasion was this:

"It is no vain thing for you, because it is your life." I forget the outlines of his sermon—and no wonder; as it was some 63 or 64 years ago—but I remember that he said again and again that religion was more important than any thing else in the world. And over and over again, he said with vehemence, and pretty well at the top of his voice, "religion is no indifferent! Religion is no indifferent! Religion is no indifferent!" Dear man, he wished everybody to think so. Well, my (or may I say our?) beloved friend, Mr. Williams, became the celebrated, the eloquent, and Apostolick Williams of Werne[2], the bright star of North Wales. He was, among the

---

[2] William Williams (1781-1840) attended Aberhavesp school when Richard Breeze was six. He was the 6th child of William Probert, farmer and carpenter of Cwmhyswn-ganol in Llanfachreth, Merionethshire and Jane, his wife. Williams worked as a carpenter for several years and began to preach at nineteen. Since he had very little education he went for nine months to a school at Aberhavesp, and then for four years, from 1803-1807, to the dissenting academy at Wrexham. As a result of his preaching as a student, he was invited to become the pastor of Wern and Harwood in the parish of Wrexham. He was ordained on 28 Oct 1808. He formed and supervised other churches and was one of the chief organisers of the Welsh Union which was formed in 1834 to liquidate chapel

Congregationalists, what those great lights were among the Baptists: I mean Samuel Breeze and Christmas Evans. Truly there were giants in those days.

I found my feeling very tender about this time, and my young heart was decidedly in favour of religion, though not above nine or ten years of age. It grieved me much when I saw people do what was wrong, and I often wept because I did not love Jesus Christ as much as I wished, and was not a better boy myself.

My mind became much perplexed upon the subject of baptism. I could not make it out. In attending the church, I found that the font was to be filled with clear water, and the child was to be dipt in the water discreetly and warily, but if not strong enough it would suffice to pour water upon him. Again, in the Church catechism, "What is the outward and visible sign in Baptism? Answer: Water; *wherein* the person is baptized in the name of the Father, and of the Son, and of the Holy Ghost." In the chapel I saw no font, only a small basin and a little water in it, and with a few drops of it the minister sprinkled the face of the child. This sent me to the New Testament. There I read of the baptism of Christ, of the Eunuch, and of John baptizing in Enon, near to Salim, because there was much water there.[3] I asked some of my friends if there were any people now who did

---

debts. He made several preaching tours throughout Wales and became renowned for his preaching.

In 1836 he became pastor of the Welsh Tabernacle in Liverpool, but returned to Wern after three years in broken health. His wife had died in 1836 and his eldest daughter in 1840. He himself died on 17 March 1841. His eldest son died, also of consumption, in 1841. A memorial column was erected in Wern in 1884. His two other children emigrated to Australia.

He is considered to have been one of the greatest Welsh preachers. His sermons were noted for their clarity and the appropriateness of the illustrations. Few were published; most were believed to be composed as he travelled on horseback from place to place. *[Dictionary of National Biography]*

[3] The following texts all imply baptism by immersion: "After baptism Jesus came up out of the water at once, and at that moment heaven opened..." *[Matthew 3:13, New English Bible]*

"'Look,' said the eunuch, 'here is water: what is there to prevent my being baptized?'; and he ordered the carriage to stop. Then they both went down into the water, Philip and the eunuch; and he baptized him. When they came up out of the water..." *[Acts 8:36, NEB]*

"John too was baptizing at Aenon, near to Salim, because water was plentiful in that region; and people were constantly coming for baptism" *[John 3:23, NEB]*

baptize in rivers as formerly. I was told that there were at Newtown, and that the Revd John Jones baptized many persons in the river Severn, and in other waters.

"Well," said I, "if I ever become a Christian I will find them out." Thus I became a Baptist, when young, unsophisticated, and untaught, except the instruction I received from the *Book of Common Prayer*, and the New Testament.

Suffer the little children to come unto me. Mark 10th. 14

> Permit them to approach, he cries,
> Nor scorn their humble name;
> For it was to bless such souls as these,
> The Lord of Angels came.

3

REMOVAL TO ANOTHER FARM. CLOGE

THE PARISH WHICH we have just now left is called Aberhavesp: aber-brook, hav-summer, esp-dry, "Brooksummerdry" parish. The brook is so often dry in summer that the water is nearly lost among the pebbles. But when we have mountain showers, or a rapid thaw, it rushes down most furiously, as noisy and turbid as a brook can well be.

This parish is called Llanwonog, or Wonog's parish, the saint, it is supposed, to whom the Church was dedicated. Cloge is high hill, because the homestead is in a dent or basin on the side of the hill.

From the front door of the house you have a very extensive view: south east, the vale of Severn; south west, the Treveglios hills; due south, you have a high mountain; north, a high hill. To ascend this last hill on a fine, clear day you have about as bold and extensive a view as any in the kingdom. Go up early on a summer's morning to see the sun rise. Good Mr. Jay of Bath always said that it was good for health to get up early to see the rising sun; that it was better than medicine; that the sun is a good doctor if people meet him just as he comes out of his eastern chamber. Mr. Jay was an early riser himself, and it is said that one winter morning a policeman was passing by his house at 4 o'clock, and, seeing a light in the cellar drew near to the grating, shouting, "What be ye at there?" The good man was busy splitting wood for the servants to light the fire. He came to the front door and said to the guardian of the night, "all right." The man then walked off, saying, "all right, Zur."

Now suppose yourself for once on the top of this mountain at 4 o'clock. Look to the east, you see the sun rise in great majesty, the king of day rejoicing as a strong man to run a race. He looks like a huge red ball of burning fire. Snowdon appears hard by, and other mountains, like subordinate officers around the general, as if ready to pay their suit to the monarch of day. Then look southeast, as far as your sight can carry you, you see the Longments, Brythen Hills and Raikins, near Shrewsbury. A little more to the south you see Rodney's pillar, and even some glimpses of Ludlow Castle. You see the smoke ascend from Newtown, when the maidens and the good housewives kindle up their morning fires. Bear off again to the southwest and you see the smoke from the town of Llanidloes begin to ascend, and the smoke of Llanfair shows itself. If you look to the northwest you see the celebrated Plinlimmon and Cader Idris.

I have often been delighted with the grandeur of this bold circular scenery. I can sympathise with an American traveller who once stood on the summit of Mount Carmel in Palestine. In the north he saw the hills of Galilee, the mountains of Syria, Tyre and Sidon, with Asia Minor and the Great Sea to the west, Egypt to the south, the wilderness of Arabia, and a little more to the southeast, the Dead Sea and the fords of the Jordan. Why, he was almost beside himself with delight. At another time he stood on one of the Andes in South America, amid the smoke and sounds of the Volcanic Craters, where he had a splendid view of the Pacific Ocean on the left hand, on the right, the great Atlantic, and right on to the north the Gulph [sic] of Mexico.

Dr. Raffles and his uncle, Sir Stamford Raffles stood once on Mont Blanc amid the glories of Creation. The good Doctor felt devout and with much feeling, waved his hand and said, "my Father made them all." The true Christian sees God in all his works and feels that he is never alone because the Father is with him.

> On the mountain top alone
> Or by a stream or fountain
> Lift thy Spirit up to God.
> Who can stop it mounting?

View from above Cloge.

View of one of small pools above Cloge.

As to Plinlimmon, it is reported that ages ago, somewhere about the morn of time, his lordship had five daughters. Two of them were very small and never went far from home, but the other three were more romantic, and wanted to see a little of the world. They decided to have a run to the sea. The night before they laid a wager which would get there first. Lady Severn[1] awoke first, and thought herself very fortunate, as she could choose the best land and the finest scenery for the journey. She set off by Newtown, Shrewsbury, Worcester, Gloucester, and then gaily entered the mighty waters of the Bristol Channel. Lady Wye awoke next, and felt much vexed with herself when she found that her sister was gone. She set off [by] a nearer cut right through Herefordshire.

Lady Rhydol awoke at length. But who can describe her excitement? She was almost desperate. Off she dashed like a fury in a westerly direction, through the vales and along the glens, tumbling over the rocks and away, making one summersault [sic] after another. She soon rolled gallantly into Cardigan Bay and won the wager.

When I was a student, a clergyman wrote me a respectful note, inclosing the following Welsh lines, requesting me to translate them for him in verse. I sent him the following free translation:

Migam Mogam, pa le y rhai dy
Miel heb wallt ph a waith y ti
Cynt tiff gwalt fy nghorin I
Na unionna yth feran geimion dy[1]

Zig Zag, Zig Zag, where co'st flee
Thou hairless pate? What's that to thee?
My hair will grow both strong & free
Before thy legs will straightened be.

Lord Plinlimmon's remark was unkind at best, and richly deserved. Lady Severn's keen retort–Let us hope that they will have no more unkind words, but henceforth and for ever live in peace.

---

[1] The story refers to the Rivers Severn, Wye and Rhydol

We have close at hand the spring heads of three brooks: Lyn Dee, or Blackpool, a pool without a bottom, the wise people say. A stream issues from that and enters Carne Brook, then the Severn near Cairsws. Lyn Maur, or the great pool, is about a mile long, and half a mile across. This lake sends forth a stream that passes through Llanfair and Meiford, and enters the Severn about three miles above Welshpool. Lyn Tarrw, or Bull Pool is another specimen of the marvellous, a pool without a bottom.

These waters run through our farm, and a beautiful trout stream it is. I have caught nearly a bucket of fish in a day many times. We have lots of small trout about the size of minnows, but how the fish come up here to deposit their spawn I cannot imagine, as there are two waterfalls that I know of, one within 100 yards of our house, not less than 40 feet [high]. Do they leap it, or do they march over dry land, and get up by that method? A modern traveller in South America says that some of the fish march on dry land from the Amazon, and actually climb up the trees. Once he shot at a bird in a tree, and down came a bird and a fish.

One time, I was passing over this mountain top on a very stormy day. The lightning flashed vividly and frightfully, the thunder rolled and echoed from hill to hill. One thunderclap seemed to explode over my head, and off I ran over the heather towards home; but, through the unevenness of the ground, and my great hurry I sprained my ankle, so I had to get home in the best way I could. Nevertheless this was a rich treat. Never did I witness any thing so awfully grand before or since, and I never shall forget it.

The exhibitor at St. Paul's names the various monuments in succession till he comes and stands under the spacious dome, then looks up and points to a Latin inscription, *Si Monumentum Requiris Circumspice.* If you wish to see his monument, look up.

That magnificent Cathedral was erected by Sir Christopher Wren. It was conceived by his great mind, raised up by his skill, and stands a monument to his greatness.

Does the fop say there is no God? Let him stand on this hill and look round, then read his own character on the holy page, and feel ashamed of himself. "The fool hath said in his heart there is no God." Again I say if you wish to see the great God in his works, look around you.

These hills are delightful for a summer residence, and would suit an unsocial recluse to admiration in the winter. There is a small village, or a cluster of small houses occupied by small freeholders, each house having a few acres of land attached to it, situated on the west side of the farm called Bwlch y Garreg, or a cleft between the rock, through which the above little stream passes.

The religious state of the neighbourhood was very bad when we came there. The distance to the Church is not less than four miles, and about one mile and a half is down a hill as steep, almost, as the side of a house. To go there and back to one service only was a good day's work. It is true that we had a blessing worth going for when we went. The worthy Curate, the Revd D. James, was a good man, and preached the gospel, so we attended as often as we could. There were religious services held in houses in the vale below, which we occasionally attended. Many thanks to the good Dissenters for the kind efforts they made to meet the moral wants of the people.

The villagers close at hand were morally in a very pitiable condition, perhaps not one praying man or woman among them all. God saw their destitute state, and moved the hearts of good people to come to their help. The Calvinistic Methodists, a large body of very useful people who have been a great blessing to the Principality, came to preach in a house in the place and to open a Sunday School.

This was indeed the beginning of a new era. The Sun of Righteousness began to shine on this benighted people. We found a pleasure in doing what we could to encourage this new undertaking. In this there was a serious difficulty; the young people did not understand the Welsh language. The service and the school were conducted in that language. We were invited to go to the school to learn it, that we might afterward become teachers. I went and began to learn my letters. I did learn, and my progress was such that on the third Sabbath I was seen reading in the Bible class. In a Sabbath or two more I had the charge of a Welsh class of children, which exercise I continued more or less till I left home to enter upon the battle of life.

Some time before I left home we had a serious family illness. We all had it except father. It proved to be the typhus fever, and that of a most malignant kind. The life of each one, when the fever was at its height, was despaired of. I was brought exceedingly low, and had no hope of recovery. I felt very much alarmed at the thought of dying. It is true that, if compared with most boys of my age, I might be said to be a good moral boy, but my deep impression was this, that I was not in a fit state to die. I had light to know that a change of heart was necessary, and that I had not felt that change.

I wept and prayed night and day, and in my mind made the most solemn promises to God, that if he would restore me to health, and give me longer time to repent, I would serve him faithfully and for ever. I meant all this, and was as sincere as an earnest and truthful spirit could be. I believed then, and even now believe it, that God did pity my tears, and hear my prayers. The fever took a favourable turn. I felt more comfortable, both in mind and body. I felt really happy, as thankful as a grateful spirit could be in my weak mortal state. I was mercifully restored, and thought that nothing could tempt me to break my promises so solemnly made. Alas! for poor human nature, and for resolutions made in my own strength. I most ungratefully went further off from God than ever I had done before, but I never could escape from my conscience.

Some time after this I was informed that there was to be a baptizing at Cairsws in the river Severn. I was pleased to hear this, as I had wished to see the ordinance administered for the last years. On the Sabbath morning I started off alone, full of mingled feelings of interest and curiosity. As I drew near to the crowded and orderly assembly, the first thought that passed my mind was this, that I was come right to the banks of the Jordan. There was the flowing river. Here were the crowds on its banks. There were the repenting Jews come to baptism, and there was John the Baptist, in the person of that dear man, the Revd John Jones of Newtown, whom I some time afterwards loved as a dear father in Jesus Christ. Nature had done much for that great and good man. He stood about six feet high, portly in person, with a fine, beaming countenance, a voice as musical as a trumpet; and with that majesty of attitude which always demanded the most respectful attention from the listening thousands, who often attended his ministry on occasions similar to the present.

We were frequently confined to home on the Sabbath day, being so far from the Church, and the weather was often stormy on the hills, but when this was the case, father would have us put on our Sabbath attire and read the Bible or some useful books. He said it was the way to improve ourselves, and to show a reverence for the sanctity of the holy day. It was also his custom on the Sabbath evening to have the whole family to read in class, each a verse, he at the head of it with his great Welsh Bible taking his turn, and he was the best reader, too, from what I can recollect. It gave us lessons in the Welsh language also, as we could see the difference in the languages.

My dear father wished me to be a miller and mealman, to which I had at the time no objection. It was arranged for me to go to a Mr. M___, a friend of his, who lived some three miles off. Mr. and Mrs. M___ were good kind of people, and well-to-do in the world. He was a calm, rational kind of man, and she was a first rate housewife, as keen as a razor, a true friend to her favourites–and those who were not must do the best they could. I came in on the sunny side, and did very well.

A few years after this I was invited by the mourners to conduct a religious service at the funeral of this dear woman, and we found it to be a solemn and profitable season.

One incident which happened during my stay with these good people I ought not to pass over. It was my habit at times to go home on Saturday nights and to return on the morrow evening. One evening I did not go home. That night we retired to rest at the usual time. About one o'clock I heard a shrill unnatural call, somewhat like a man trying to imitate a female voice.

"Mr. and Mrs. M___, come down immediately. Your son lies a-dying." I thought there was something wrong, but did not speak. I prepared myself for the worst. I braced up my nerves and listened, heard the old people go downstairs, and the servant girl helping them off. Just then a little grandchild who slept with the servant cried out in bed. I heard the young woman hurry upstairs, and as she went down with the child on her arm I heard a voice in suppressed tones ask if young Breeze was in bed. My worst fears were aroused, and I jumped up and through the door, when I heard some one run down the stairs–and I ran after him; but before I reached the door

I could hear the would-be robber run up the yard with all his might. I then lectured the girl for not having shut the front door after letting the good people out. Her reply was this, that she was afraid the child would fall off the bed, that as she came to the top of the stairs a rush of wind from the front door put out the candle. Coming down a few steps more in the dark she put her hand on a man's head, who whispered the words named above. Then she went down to try to light the candle, and was so engaged when the fellow escaped. The door being shut and locked I took hold of the poker, and said to the girl, "Follow me."

We went through the house but found no one. Then we heard a number of people run down the yard, the old lady first in the race, she came right to the door, which opened.

"Oh, dear," said she, "is the house robbed?"

I said, "no."

She flew up stairs and was soon down again, and, with an agitated countenance said, "Alright. How was it?" and when I told her and the rest my tale, she said, "What a merciful deliverance!" There were present, the old people, the son, his wife and all the servants, the distance being not above the fourth of a mile. I saved them, no doubt, the loss of £500 or £600. The old gentleman had done some business of late years in purchasing spade guineas[2], each at the time was worth several shillings above their former standard value. He had also the rents of some of his friends with his own, that he had to pay over on the following Monday. Well, they forgot to make me a handsome present for my valour, and I, most likely, did not trouble myself about it.

The good people kept their cash in an old-fashioned large plum tree tea caddy placed on a chest of drawers in their own bedroom. If the fellow knew this, which most likely he did, he might have carried it off with the greatest ease had I not been in the way. I may state, that a few years before, the same house had been robbed. The robber was then taken and condemned to transportation.

---

[2] From 1787 to 1799, guineas and half-guineas were nicknamed spade guineas because of the shape of the royal shield used on the reverse during those years. [Chapman, Colin, *How Heavy, How Much and How Long*, Dursley, GLS, Lochin, 1995.]

A Parental Prayer

Father of all! before thy throne
Grateful but anxious parents bow;
Look in paternal mercy down
And yield the boon we ask thee now.

Tis not for wealth, or joys of earth
Or life prolonged we seek thy face
Tis for a new and heavenly birth
Tis for the treasures of thy grace

Tis for their souls' eternal joy,
For rescue from the coming woe,
Do not our earnest suit deny;
We cannot, cannot let thee go.

4

Going to Reside at Newtown

I HAD FOR some time a secret desire in my heart to learn the flannel manufacturing business. I was at length apprenticed, to my great satisfaction. I used to think that no town was equal to Newtown, somewhat like the young woman who lately said,

"I am a native of Pontypool, the most beautifullest city in the world."

I do not feel disposed at present to dispute the statement. Still Newtown is to me a very beautiful city indeed. It became the place of my second birth, and of a thousand pleasing associations besides. The varied scenery in the locality is truly enchanting. I have stood on Bryn Hill on the day of a fair and looked upon the town, the bridge, the wide street up to the old market house, and the roads leading into the town, all crowded with men and women and cattle, horses &c. It may be said to be a commercial and bustling town, with a population of some 9,000 people. Take your stand on this hill on a winter evening about 8 o'clock, when the houses and the factories are lighted up, and you will witness an unusually dazzling sight that will repay your journey up the steep ascent.

That the scenery around is very lovely is certain. In this opinion I am not alone. In reading the *Typography [sic] of Wales* by T. Evans Esq., a book that every Welshman especially ought to possess, I was pleased to meet with the following description of the beloved locality:

> "Returning to our road, at the distance of about 8 miles from Montgomery, we pass through Newtown, or Tre-Newydd, a neat town, built after the Welsh fashion, and situate in a beautiful valley, enriched by the Severn, with meadows and pastures and bounded on each side of the

river by moderate hills, generally mantled with wood, which cannot fail to render it a delightful situation for a residence–possessing every requisite for good society and amusements; without the bustle, luxury and dissipation of larger towns."

> Thus far from cities let me flee;
> Far from the crowded seat
> Of folly, pageantry and power,
> To this beloved retreat.
>
> Here plenty sheds with liberal hand
> Her various blessings round;
> Here pleasing mirth delighted roved,
> And roseate health is found.
>
> Miss James.

There are several woollen manufactories contiguous to this town, and many new dwellings, taking the place of those formed of laths and plaster.

The Church is an antique edifice consisting of a nave and chancel, having in the latter a marble table, and in the wall close by a small monument for Sir John Pryce, Bart. Near it is an elegant gilt partition in the church, containing various curious devices, and an antique font, reported to have been brought from Abbey Cromhir, Radnorshire. Near the town is an extensive park, and an ancient seat of the Pryces, who were the lineal descendants of one of the royal tribes of North Wales. Now I may add, in 1867, that a new church has been erected, and several large chapels: the Baptist Chapel seats about 1,200 people; the Wesleyan Chapel seats nearly that number; the Calvinistic Methodist Chapel about 900; the Independent Chapel full 700; and the Primitive Methodist Chapel, say 500.

It is called Newtown, some say, because the old town was burnt down and the present was built on the same site and, that while digging foundations for houses, much ash was turned up, as is supposed, from the ruins of the old town.

In the above quotation it is said to be a "neat town, built after the Welsh fashion." This statement may be objectionable, as it is generally supposed that both Newtown and Llanidloes were built by the Romans, and that in the form of a cross, as they generally built their towns after the days of Constantine the Great.

That the Romans did bear considerable sway in this part of Wales there can be no doubt, and that the city of Caersws with its camps and Roman road might be a central station. But all is conjecture at best. What a rich treat it would be to see a truthful history of these localities, now so deeply hidden in mystery.

I felt pleased with my new undertaking, and made respectable progress in acquiring a knowledge of the business. I became associated with several respectable young men; and, I believe, was much respected by them. Mr. Samuel Evans, a truly good young man was one of them. He was clever in the business, and had then commenced to manufacture goods on his own account. This young man became one of the most practical manufacturers of flannels in the town, also one of the most useful members of the Baptist Church, and did for many years sustain the office of Deacon in that church with great honour.

He wished to form an acquaintance with the London drapers, and, knowing that it was my intention to begin business myself after I had a little more experience, and, in other respects, found it convenient to do so, he proposed that I should go with him to London to sell flannels on commission. After consulting my parents on the subject, and finding no opposition on their part, as they had confidence in me, and the highest confidence in my friend, we agreed, therefore, to go.

We were certainly surprised, and much flattered at the willingness of the manufacturers to entrust us with their goods. We really might have had goods to an unlimited extent. One gentleman, a little more careful than the rest, asked me to give him security. I said in reply that my father was prepared to do it if required. He answered, "All right."

Having selected our goods, and sent off the heavy bales by the canal, we were influenced by a thought of rather a romantic character, which was to walk to Shrewsbury–33 miles–at the expense of sixpence each. We went to Welshpool, a little more than a third of the distance, where we spent all that we had allowed ourselves. We resumed our journey, but were obliged to draw up within three miles of the end, weary and foot-sore. We agreed to be boys no longer, as our undertaking was a very responsible one, and required us to act the part of men. After a rest and refreshment we soon arrived at the town, retired to rest, were called up at 4 o'clock in the morning, and at five we found ourselves on the top of a London coach on a wretchedly cold day a little before Christmas.

I had provided myself with a small bottle of gin. It just filled my waistcoat pocket, from which I took a few drops of comfort every now and then. Bad philosophy bye the bye; if fermented drinks tend to open the pores of the skin, the cold winds get into your system more easily. No man in his senses would think of throwing open the doors of his house on a cold night to keep himself warmer, but will shut them all carefully. An old coachman told me once that a glass of cold water always made him warmer when driving through the cold than a glass of spirits. Be that as it may, I found on arriving at Coventry that my little bottle wanted replenishing; and I went up to the bar of an hotel to have it filled. At the sound of the horn we were all up in our places and away. A merry young fellow sat by my side. It seemed as if he came into the world on purpose to tell tales, and then to laugh at them. He was suddenly taken seriously ill–so he said. We all had our sympathies. Oh, such pain in the stomach. Some said that he had talked too much, but most of them ascribed it to the severe weather. At length I thought of my flask. Yes, and right glad I was that I had by me so potent a remedy. So, I, in my simplicity, drew it out of my pocket and handed it to him, saying, "Please, Sir, to drink a portion of my gin," and did not I feel proud that I was able to relieve suffering humanity. He grasped it eagerly, as if it were a matter of life and death with him, drank it up, every drop, and with a hearty laugh said, "I am cured already. What first-rate gin," and he handed me back the empty bottle with a "Thank-you, Sir."

I found that I was done; and he most likely thought it a good joke. I too might have thought it not much amiss either if he had refilled my bottle with comforts at the next inn, but no, thank you, he changed his quarters and went inside the coach, perhaps lest I might feel disposed to return the joke. I was, in fact, more amused than angry with the fellow. Still I thought to return the compliment in some way or other if he had ventured to come within my reach. We arrived at the "Bull and Mouth" in the city of London at eight o'clock in the morning, half frozen to death.

Our first object was to get a comfortable breakfast, then to find a safe and convenient lodging. We found this in St. Martin's Lane.

The next thing in order was to get the goods there. So we went to the *Castle and Falcon*, and from thence we had them conveyed to our quarters, where they were placed in order of sale. Then we furnished ourselves with patterns of the respective pieces and went forth to make our calls upon the drapers. Some would come to the warehouse to inspect them, and make their selections out of the stock. Others might say, send in so many pieces of such and such a pattern &c. So with calls at various places we succeeded to sell nearly all our stock, take the money and deposit it as we received it, in the Bank of Glyn and Co., Burchin Lane.

The last few pieces we sold very cheap, that we might return the sooner. The customer was rather hard upon us; but when paying the money he made a mistake, by giving us one pound note too much. We detected the mistake, and in speaking to each other in a Welsh whisper, we fully agreed, although he had dealt hardly with us, not to take advantage of his incorrect reckoning. When informed of it he would scarcely believe us; but counting it over again he found that we were right.

He looked at us and said, "Now if you come up next year, call upon me first, and I will give you more for your goods than I will give any one else". A gentleman standing by said, "Sir, if you had had any persons here except Welshmen or Scotchmen, you would have lost that pound note."

They were pleased with us, and we were not a little pleased with ourselves for once. Honesty is the best policy all the world over. No business was done in the Christmas week owing to stock taking, pleasure taking, &c.

We had time to visit friends from the country, and to see some of London Sights. During our stay we went to hear several able Ministers; Dr. Rippon, Rowland Hill[1], &c. We had been cautioned against the London

---

[1] Rowland Hill, 1744-1833, was the sixth son of Sir Rowland Hill, first baronet. He received deep religious impressions through the conversation and letters of his brother Richard. He met scorn at St. John's College, Cambridge due to his religious views and

sharpers; and a good thing it was, as we were tried by many of them; and they found us too sharp to be turned into flats. A party called me aside one day and whispered that they had just come up from Deal, had a large quantity of smuggled goods, Indian silks, &c. and that they would let me have them for the next thing to nothing. Another time a fellow begged of my friend to buy a watch of him, as he was in great distress, and must either sell or starve. He would let it go at one pound, and it would fetch five pounds any day. My friend was, for the moment, off his guard, and offered him the money. No, said the fellow, let us go into an inn and have a glass over the deal. Just then a lady came and whispered to me, "Those are bad men, Sir. Have nothing to do with them." For by this time several had placed themselves around us, all dressed in sailor's attire. We, however, got away, with some difficulty, unhurt.

Several persons told me that I must go to a theatre before I left town. I asked my friend if he would go.

"Certainly not," was the reply, "and I hope you will not go." This was the answer I fully expected from him. Nothing would induce him to go to what he called the 'Devil's House'. A true man he was, firm as a rock. A friend of mine offered to go with me; and so we went to Covent Garden Theatre. I did not find it to be a school of virtue. In coming out through the crowd my friend lost the hind quarter of his coat. What a wretched sight at the doors; rogues, shrimps, strumpets, pickpockets &c. This was my first and last visit to a theatre and if I were to live in this world a thousand years it would, doubtless, be my last.

---

earnest efforts to do good. He visited prisoners and the sick, preached in Cambridge and the adjoining villages and was often insulted by mobs. After graduation six bishops refused to grant him orders owing to his unorthodox activities. Finally in 1773 the bishop of Bath and Wells ordained him to the curacy of Kingston, Somersetshire. He was most diligent in his parochial duties but at the same time continued to make extensive evangelistic tours. He was refused priest's orders on account of his irregularities. He continued to preach wherever he could find an audience. A chapel was built for him at Wotton, Gloucestershire and he officiated here for a part of every year. In 1783, Surrey Chapel, London, was built for him and from that time he primarily preached here. His sermons attracted large congregations. Thirteen Sunday schools with over 3,000 children were attached to the chapel. He published many religious works and took a prominent part in most of the religious and philanthropic movements of the time. He died 11 April 1833 and was buried beneath the pulpit of Surrey Chapel. *[Dictionary of National Biography]*

In due time we returned home, and put all our affairs straight, to the perfect satisfaction of all with whom we had to do. We felt truly thankful to God for his kind protection, and our friends were glad for our safe return.

Soon after our return from London my esteemed friend Mr. Evans was baptized. This was to me the beginning of a new and blissful era. On the morning of a Sabbath day in the presence of a large concourse of people, my friend, with some other candidates, was baptized by the beloved pastor, Mr. Jones, in the River Severn. When Mr. Evans was going down into the water these words sounded in my ears,

"Two shall be together in the field. The one shall be taken and the other left."[2] Now where these words came from I cannot tell, not even to this day. I may have heard them from the lips of the Minister; or whether the Holy Spirit suggested them to my mind; or it may have been the voice of an enlightened conscience reminding me of my dangerous condition. The effect of the words was awful. It seemed as if it were my death warrant. My friend was saved, and I was left. I cried aloud and wept, and prayed for mercy, as if the great Judge were on his throne about to pronounce the sentence of condemnation, "Depart ye cursed."

I never felt anything like this before. I followed the good people to the chapel and witnessed the candidates received into the Church and the administration of the Lord's Supper. I could do nothing but weep and hear the awful words over and over again, "Two shall be, &c." I was in this hopeless and distressed state of mind for above two months. Truly wretched in the day time, and at night I had but little sleep. When I dozed for a short time I was scared with terrible dreams. One night I dreamed that the judgement day was come and the mountains were on fire, that volcanic eruptions sent forth columns of fire into the air, and all of them were directed towards me. At one time I thought I stood in one of my father's fields. I thought I saw an immense number of evil spirits, creatures that resembled goats, or monkeys. They all advanced towards me and,

---

[2] "That is how it will be when the Son of Man comes. Then there will be two men in the field; one will be taken, the other left; two women grinding at the mill; one will be taken, the other left." *[Matthew 24, 39-41, New English Bible]*

when the horrible things came near, I fell on my knees to beg of God to protect me from them. In looking again I found them retreating, and the more earnestly I prayed, the more they disappeared.

One night I thought myself on a narrow ridge, with deep, black ditches on each hand, and a great number of persons wading in the black waters, trying in vain to get out. The sight was dreadful to behold. I felt certain that I should fall in; and a good thought came to my help. It was that I should travel on my hands and knees. I obeyed the suggestion, and did, through mercy, with great difficulty pass over this dangerous place. I have often, in the morning, found my pillow wet with my tears.

Still these horrible visions of the night were full of instruction. I learned this great secret, that if I conquered my foes at all it must be on my knees. God's help was to be secured at a throne of grace. It could be found there, and there I found it at last to the joy of my soul.

The thought came often to my mind at this time that there was no need of my despairing to obtain favours, that there were many young men in the town ten times worse than I, and that some very bad ones had become good men, and why not I be saved?

I never was a profligate. I hated swearing, drunkenness, lying, and all mean and base practices. Why not hope, and even thank God that I was not as other men, but no, these thoughts brought no comfort to my troubled mind. I felt that I was unfit to die, and not worthy to live on God's earth. I felt I was not only unholy but sin itself; every thought was evil and that continually.

My broken promises grieved me exceedingly. I felt that I had been mocking God, and could not for shame ask his mercy. Nor could I dare to promise a reformation, for I had no confidence in myself. To continue vowing and promising and then breaking all when the least temptation came in my way, was only adding sin to sin.

I could not pursue my calling and made up my mind to go among my relatives for a few weeks, either to find comfort, or to shake off these wretched forebodings and to brace up my nerves to meet with hardened fortitude the dark future, whatever that future might be. In my wicked and deceitful heart I secretly hoped to find in my friends a people full of fun and vanity, which would help to cheer me up, and drive dull cares away. But no, I found them quite the reverse to this. The first family I visited was truly a pious family. Uncle, Aunt and cousins formed a happy and a pious group of saints. In a day or two they invited me to go with them to a farmhouse to hear preaching. We went together. The minister was very earnest and eloquent. His subject was, "There is joy in heaven over one sinner that repenteth, more than over ninety and nine just persons that need no repentance." I do not remember the sermon, but I think it was as follows: He said that holy angels were delighted to see sinners saved; God was delighted to see sinners saved and made happy; the Church was delighted to see sinners saved; every creature in God's universe would feel delighted in the salvation of sinners except wicked men and wicked devils. From this subject there was comfort to the penitent and sorrow to the hardened sinner who would not be saved.

Strange to say, my impression was this, that devils would rejoice in my damnation. I felt so morbid and unbelieving, yet my tears flowed freely and I could not stop them nor conceal them.

My friends saw my distress, and spoke to me in a very kind and encouraging manner. Wherever I called I found the good people very religious and all urged me kindly to give myself to Jesus Christ, and to his service, and take heed not to resist the Spirit; that God was willing to save me or he would not follow me up with such deep and painful convictions.

I thought there was right reason in this. I took heart, and tried to look to Christ by faith, and did really begin to feel more comfortable. I returned at length to my father's house with a heart less sad, and with a countenance more cheerful. I felt now determined in my own mind to be the Lord's for ever.

Monday came, and I had to return to town. In doing so, I called upon my sister Jane. She and her husband were good Christian people.[3] I told her of all my troubles and hopes, asking her advice. It was this; to go home in time for the church meeting at the Baptist Chapel, to call upon Mr. A__

---

[3] **Jane Brees**, bap 14 March 1790 *[Llanwnog BT]*; married Samuel Jones, bachelor, both of this parish, by banns, 25 April 1810 *[Aberhafesp Bishop's Transcripts]*

in my road, a young man I knew, and a member of the Church; that he would be pleased to introduce me.

I felt, however, that it would be a formidable undertaking, but thought I would go. As I was passing through Aberhavesp Hall meadows, I went aside to a hedge to pray to God for strength, and while thus engaged with much earnestness a bird fluttered in the hedge, and drove me away. Then my foolish heart told me that God sent it there on purpose, because he would not hear my chattering noise. However I still thought I would go, and if God would have mercy upon me he would shew it by keeping the young man at home till I reached his house. Here I was again disappointed. The young man was gone before I arrived. This was a proof to me that there was no hope for me in God. In this way I continued to be tormented by doubts and fears and temptations for several weeks. At length relief came. Some of the good people attending the Baptist Chapel hearing of my troubles called upon me, spoke to me words of comfort, and invited me to attend the experience meetings. I did so, and felt delighted with the kindness and sympathy of the good people. I felt that I had been trying to save myself instead of going to Jesus Christ just as I was. I found out the great evangelical doctrine, Free Salvation through Christ, Justification by Faith.

> Nothing in my hand I bring
> Simply to thy cross I cling

Yes, and could say:

> I'm a poor sinner and nothing at all,
> But Jesus Christ is my all in all.

I became happy, very happy in my mind and longed to follow Jesus in his holy ordinances, and to become one with his people. I was received as a candidate for baptism at the next Church meeting.

These were my feelings at that time, beautifully and correctly expressed:

Dear Lord and will thy pardoning love
Embrace a wretch so vile?
Will thou my load of guilt remove
And bless me with thy smile?

Hast thou the cross for me endured
And all the shame despised?
And shall I be ashamed, O Lord
With thee to be baptized?

Didst thou the great example lead
In Jordan's swelling flood?
And shall my pride disdain the deed
That's worthy of my God?

Dear Lord, the ardour of thy love
Reproves my cold delays,
And now my willing footsteps move
In thy delightful ways.

5

BAPTISM AND THE BAPTISTS

THE HAPPY DAY at length arrived, and it was indeed a happy day. I believe it was one of the happiest days I ever spent on earth. I do not believe in baptismal regeneration nor that we can merit anything at the hand of Jesus Christ by any of our doings, but I have no doubt of this, that, "In keeping his commandments there is great reward."

There was a large body of people at my baptism. Some were old friends who had come some distance. Some were pleased, and others wondered what all this meant.

The Baptists were a numerous and respectable body of people in this neighbourhood. The first in the field, they have proved a great blessing to tens of thousands of precious souls.

It will be pleasant and profitable to review the history of the Baptists for the last 200 years in this highly favoured portion of the Lord's vineyard.

The first Baptist minister who preached the gospel in this neighbourhood was the famous Vavasor Powell.[1] This eminent Minister was born at

---

[1] Vavasor Powell was born in 1617 at Cnweglas or Knuclas in the parish of Heyop, Radnorshire. At age seventeen, his uncle, Erasmus Howell, vicar of Clun, Shropshire, sent him to Jesus College, Oxford. He left without a degree and became a schoolmaster at Clun and also his uncle's curate and as 'a reader of common prayer.' By 1639 his deepening religious convictions led him to become an itinerant evangelist. An independent income made this possible.

His first arrest, as Richard Breeze notes, was in 1640 in Breconshire. [Insert note on why he was arrested--unclear] On the surrender of Raglan Castle to Parliament by the Royalists in August 1646, Powell returned to Wales. As well as his preaching throughout Wales he was 'pastor' of the church at Newtown, Montgomeryshire. His religious position at this time was as an independent.

Cnweglas in Radnorshire in the year 1617. He was related to some of the most respectable families in the counties of Radnor, Montgomery and Salop. After undergoing a suitable preparatory training in the country he entered Jesus College, Oxford, where he is said to have made considerable proficiency in the various branches of literature. On his return from the University he kept a school for some time, at Clun, in Shropshire. His uncle, Erasmus Powell, being the incumbent of that parish, used to assist him in reading the prayers &c, but though well educated, and in holy orders, and having entered the ministry in the Established Church, he was, till the his age [*sic*] an utter stranger to spiritual religion, a vain and thoughtless youth, and even a ringleader amongst his associates in folly and wickedness. But the Spirit of the Lord graciously, and somewhat unexpectedly arrested him in his sinful career.

On one Lord's day, probably after reading prayers at Church, he was standing in his clerical dress or, as he terms it, the habit of a foolish shepherd, looking at a number of people breaking the Sabbath by divers games. One of those people called Puritans, accidentally passing by, mildly addressed him,

"Doth it become you, Sir, who are a Scholar, and one that teacheth others to break the Lord's day thus?"

To which he replied, like the scoffers in Malachi,[2] "Wherein do I break, &c. You see me only stand by. I do not play at all."

The recognition of Cromwell as Lord Protector in 1653 split the independents. Powell himself preached against the 'usurpation'. By 1654 he moved to the baptist section of the independents and was preaching against the baptism of infants. His popularity as a preacher remained high. The authorities suspected him of being a leader of anti-Cromwell insurgents, though Powell took no part in political struggles.

He is said to be the first non-conformist in trouble after the Restoration in 1660, principally on account of his preaching [specifically?] When brought up at the assizes he refused to take the oath of allegiance and supremacy on the grounds that these were meant for papists.

Richard Breeze has summarized his subsequent career. [*Dictionary of National Biography*]

[2] The only quotation from Malachi that seems appropriate here is the following:

"You have said, [said the Lord] 'it is useless to serve God; what do we gain from the Lord of Hosts by observing his rules and behaving with deference? We ourselves count the arrogant happy; it is evildoers who are successful; they have put God to the proof and come to no harm." [*Malachi 3:14, New English Bible*]

"But," replied he, "you find your own pleasure herein by looking on; and this God forbids in his holy word."

So he opened his bible and read these words in Isaiah, 58-13[3], particularly that expression, "not finding thine own pleasure, upon the Sabbath day." The words had such an effect upon his mind that he resolved never to transgress in that way again. And God enabled him to abide by his resolution. But he was not yet thoroughly convinced of his lost state by nature, and his need of Christ. This took place in the year 1638. About a year after, Providence led him to hear "an excellent old preacher", probably Mr. Wroth whose words left an indelible impression upon his mind, which was subsequently deepened by reading Gibb's bruised Reed [sic], and one of Mr. Perkins's works. At length, through the powerful ministry of Mr. Walter Cradock, and various other means, he was led to surrender himself entirely to God. The exact time when he began to preach is not certainly known. In the year 1640 when preaching at a house in Brecknockshire, he and about fifty or sixty of his hearers were seized by fifteen or sixteen persecutors, who pretended that they had a warrant from one Justice Williams of Builth. That night they were locked up in a Church, and the next day conducted to the justice, who committed them to the hands of the constables. The following day they were examined before several justices, and six or seven clergymen, but after a long discussion they were at that time dismissed with many threats. Some time after, when preaching in a field, in Radnorshire, to a large congregation, Mr. Powell was arrested, and committed, by his kinsman, Mr. Hugh Lloyd, the high sheriff. The sixteen or seventeen constables who were charged with the execution of the *mittimus*, all, except one, would have nothing to do with it. This man, taking Mr. Powell to his own house, which was on the way, and permitting him to lodge there that night because the prison was at a great distance, was so affected with his devotions in the family that he could proceed no further.

---

[3] "If you cease to tread the sabbath underfoot, and keep my holy day free from your own affairs, if you call the sabbath a day of joy and the Lord's holy day a day to be honoured, if you honour it by not plying your trade, not seeking your own interest or attending to your own affairs, then you shall find your joy in the Lord, and I will set you riding on the heights of the hearth, and your father Jacob's patrimony shall be yours to enjoy; the Lord himself has spoken it." [*New English Bible,* Isaiah 58, 13-14]

He left the prisoner in his own house, and absconded, but the persecuted minister, to prevent any trouble to the constable, bound himself with two sureties to appear at the next assizes for Radnorshire. At the assizes he was honourably acquitted of the charges preferred against him, and to the great mortification of his persecutors he was invited to dine with the judge. The high sheriff, however, continued implacable, and did not rest until he had persecuted him out of the country. To save his life he fled to London, where he arrived in August 1641. He remained in England four years and six months. For the first two years he preached in London and, for the last two years and six months, at Dartford in Kent. He was remarkably popular and useful at Dartford.

As soon as the storm of war was over some of the members of the church in Radnorshire went all the way to Kent to invite their beloved pastor to return to them. Before his return he appeared to be examined by the Committee of the Assembly of Divines appointed to examine and approve public preachers. Some of the Committee proposed that he should receive Presbyterian ordination, but, being a firm Congregationalist, and, as such, entertaining doubts whether a Committee of ministers had power to ordain a person without the consent of the church over which he was to exercise his ministry, he would not admit it. After some debate between him and Mr. Stephen Marshall in particular, it was agreed to waive the objection, and grant him the testimonial, which was signed by seventeen of the Committee, amongst whom we find the names of Joseph Caryl, William Greenhill, Jeremiah Whitaker, Jeremiah Burroughs, Christopher Love, William Strong, Philip Key, &c.

On his return to Wales he became a most indefatigable and active instrument in propagating the gospel among his fellow countrymen. He very often preached two or three times the same day, and was seldom two days in the week, throughout the years, without preaching. There was scarcely a church, chapel, or town hall in the principality in which he had not preached. He also often preached at fairs, markets, in fields, and on the mountains, and wherever he could find a number of people to preach to. It is impossible to form an adequate idea of the extent of his labours in Wales from the year 1646 to 1660.

Mr. Powell was thoroughly conscientious; and sincerely aimed in all his movements to promote the glory of God and the salvation of men. But he did not act with such prudence and caution as to secure the objects he had in view.

His becoming a Baptist, and his sympathy with the Quakers, lowered him in the estimation of some people.[4]

On the 20 April 1660 a company of soldiers entered his house, and dragged him to prison at Welshpool, from which place he was soon removed to Shrewsbury, where he was kept a prisoner for about nine weeks, and then, by an order from the King and Council, he and his fellow prisoners were relieved.

On his release from Shrewsbury jail he returned to Wales, and to the great and most delightful work of his life, preaching the gospel to his fellow countrymen. But the high sheriff of Montgomeryshire thought it his duty to prohibit him. Upon Mr. Powell's refusal to comply with that prohibition, he was again imprisoned, after enjoying his liberty for only twenty-four days. Having been detained in prison in Montgomeryshire for some months he was removed to the Fleet Prison, London, where he was kept nearly two years, closely confined in a small, unhealthy, and most offensive room. This cruel treatment so impaired his health that he never afterwards recovered. On the 30 September, 1662, he was conveyed from the Fleet Prison to Southsea Castle, near Portsmouth, and was confined there for above five years. Upon the fall of Clarendon,[5] the power of the bloody pa-

---

[4] But raised him highly in the estimation of God and all good men. (Marginal note added by the author)

[5] Edward Hyde, 1st Earl of Clarendon, was a staunch Anglican. From 1646-1660 he shared exile with Charles, Prince of Wales, later Charles II. He was created Earl of Clarendon in 1661 and dominated the administration for the next few years. He opposed the king's policy of indulgence and was the sponsor of the Clarendon Code. He did not conciliate Parliament and in 1663 there was an attempt at impeachment. In 1667 he was finally dismissed. He went into exile in France where he completed his *History of the Great Rebellion*, begun during his first exile.

The Clarendon Code included: (1) The Corporation Act, 1661, which required all municipal officeholders to take oaths of allegiance, supremacy and non-resistance &c, within 12 months of election; (2) The Act of Uniformity, 1662, required all clergy to declare their consent to everything in the Book of Common Prayer, &c.; (3) The Conventicle Act, 1664, tried to prevent clergy who had been ejected under the Act of Uniformity from

trons of persecution being somewhat reduced, Mr. Powell sued for *Habeas Corpus*; and soon after, by an order from the King and Council, obtained his liberty once more.

Scarcely ten months elapsed before he was again imprisoned. Having gone to Bath and Bristol, for the benefit of his health, on his return home he preached to large congregations in Monmouthshire. From Newport in that county he proceeded to Merthyr Tydvil, in Glamorganshire, where nearly a thousand people assembled to hear him in and about the churchyard.

He preached to them from Jeremiah XIII, 7-8.[6] While he was preaching, George Jones, the parson of the parish, a man of a most reprobate character, posted away to Cardiff, to procure authority from the Deputy-lieutenant to arrest him. Amongst other falsehoods he swore that he was accompanied by a large number of armed men. The following morning several officers, headed by one J. Carne, a Major in the County Militia, apprehended Mr. Powell at his lodgings in Merthyr Tydvil. When he desired to see their authority Carne laid his hand upon his sword and said "*that* was his authority". Being conveyed to Cardiff he was committed to the County Prison. This was about the beginning of October 1668. After several mock trials in Cardiff and Cowbridge, a friend in London procured a writ of *Habeas Corpus* to remove him to the Court of Common Pleas, which the Sheriff refused to obey, until he was threatened with a penalty of £100. On the 16 May, 1669, he left Cardiff for London, where he appeared at the Court of Common Pleas on the 22nd of the same month, and, though none of the charges against him were proved, he could not obtain his liberty, but was again committed to the Fleet Prison, merely to please his implacable en-

---

forming their own congregations. Anyone over 16 attending an unlawful conventicle was liable to a fine or imprisonment. A conventicle was a group of four, non-family members who were assembling to worship other than according to the Church of England Prayer Book.; (4) The Five Mile Act, 1665, prohibited dissenting ministers from living within five miles of any place they had served before the passage of the Act.

The Code was named after Edward Hyde, although he was not the prime instigator. *[The History Today Companion to British History]*

[6] "So I went to Perath and looked for the place where I had hidden it [the girdle], but when I picked it up, I saw that it was spoilt, and no good for anything. Again the Lord spake to me and these were his words; Thus will I spoil the gross pride of Judah, the gross pride of Jerusalem." [Jeremiah 13, 7-8, *New English Bible*]

emies. From this time he remained in prison until he was discharged by death, at four o'clock in the afternoon, October 27, 1670.

Mr. Henry Williams, pastor of the Congregational[7] Church in Montgomeryshire, a laborious and useful minister, and one of the most amiable men that ever lived, was also one of the greatest sufferers. Among the severe sufferings and heavy trials which Mr. Williams underwent the following have been related as some of the most remarkable.

He was once set upon while preaching, dragged from the place where he stood, cruelly beaten, and left apparently dead like Paul at Lystra.[8] His imprisonments were long and rigorous and are said to have taken up no less than nine years. At one of the times he lay in prison the bloody persecutors set fire to his house and burnt it to the ground. Another time they beset it, broke in and plundered his goods, and even attempted to murder his aged father who was attempting to prevent their getting into the upper rooms. His wife also, then pregnant, in endeavouring to make her escape with one child in her arms, and leading another, they cruelly insulted. At last they seized the stock upon the land, and seemed resolved to leave nothing behind them for the future subsistence of the family. There was, however a field of wheat just sown, which the unfeeling wretches could not carry off, and probably did not think it worth their while to destroy. That field thrived amazingly. All the winter and spring its appearance struck every beholder, and the crop it produced was so very abundant as to become the common talk and wonder of the whole country. Nothing like it had ever been known in those parts. In short the produce of that field amply repaid him for all the losses of the preceding year. It was said indeed that it amounted to more than double the value of what the persecuting plunderers had carried off. This, together with the untimely and awful end of several of his most bitter persecutors had such a terrifying effect upon the inhabitants as secured him from being ever afterwards so barbarously

---

[7] "Baptist" added here.

[8] Paul visited Derbe and Lystra where he found a disciple, Timothy. They travelled through Phrigia and Galatia together. In Philippi, they were imprisoned and beaten. The prison doors burst open in an earthquake and the fearful guards were baptized. They were released by the magistrates the next day. [Summarized from Acts 16, *New English Bible*]

treated. The said field, I believe, is known there, and shewn to strangers to this day.

It was not uncommon in that persecuting age for such as had been very forward and cruel in oppressing and persecuting others to be themselves overtaken by some dreadful disaster, which very much had the appearance of a divine visitation or judgement. This is said to have been remarkably the case with several of those who had been most forward, or principally concerned in oppressing this good man and his family. Two of these were justices of the peace. One of them died suddenly while he was eating his dinner. The other, as he was returning home drunk from Newtown, fell into the Severn and was drowned. Another, who was, I think, the high sheriff or his deputy, who had been active in seizing and taking away the cattle and goods of our pious sufferer, fell off his horse some time after, within sight of the injured man's house, and broke his neck.

I have heard much about Mr. H. Williams, the sufferings he passed through, and the wonderful manner in which God appeared on his behalf; how the Lord comforted him in his iron judgements. It was the common talk of the country people when I was quite a little boy. The field is often pointed out, and the farmhouse also, to persons passing by. I have heard of people coming considerable distances to see the place, and to make enquiries as to the truthfulness of the above statements. I have heard it often said that the renowned Rev^d. Vavasour Powell preached in the locality and had a church, a Baptist Church, of some 300 members; and that Mr. Henry Williams, a holy and laborious man, did all in his power to assist him in work and doctrine, and in any way in which he could be useful.

I never heard that there was a congregational Church in those parts, and that Mr. Williams was the pastor of it. I know this, that after the fierce persecution ceased in after years, the Baptists built a chapel at about a mile from Mr. Williams' house, the only chapel for many miles around, and soon afterwards chose the Rev^d. James Evans for their pastor. He was a student from the Baptist College, Bristol,[9] and father of my late esteemed

---

9 At Oxford, members of the University were required to subscribe to the Thirty-nine Articles and to take the Oath of Supremacy. At Cambridge, the rules were similar. Many of the dissenting ministers realized the damage to their churches if prospective pastors and

friend, the Revd. James Evans, Caerleon. The Independents did, some years afterwards, build a chapel at Bwlch-y-frith, about four miles off, and a great blessing it has been to the neighbourhood, and continues to be so till this day. It has my hearty good wishes. It was in that chapel I received my first religious impressions.

Newtown had been hitherto the strong citadel of the determined adversary. The Baptist forces had the honour of making the first attack upon it. It was a forlorn hope. However a breach was made, and men with brave hearts rushed in and gained possession. They hoisted the flag of liberty and love. It is for us to recount the glorious triumphs achieved since that time, all bloodless victories. A humble room was taken over a smithy, very humble and very small. A few people dared at first to come, the number increased, the room became too small. A larger one was taken in the Cross, a position much more respectable. This became too strait for the good people. One evening, owing to the crowd assembled, the timber of the house felt the pressure of the weight, and gave way with a loud report. It does not appear that any one was hurt, but all concluded that the building was not safe to be used for that purpose again.

It should be stated that a considerable revival of religion had taken place recently. Several respectable young people had been converted to God. Two young men of great promise were among the rest. One a Mr. Richard Pryce, the son of worthy parents residing in the town, became a very eminent preacher in his day. When I first knew him personally he was the worthy and much honoured Pastor of the Baptist Church at Coate, in Oxfordshire. I often called upon him, and once, when there, he told me, with much humour, about the above place of worship. That one Sabbath, when going there, a number of young men in the street linked hands, made a circle around him, and cried out at the top of their voices, "Amen, amen, amen, &c" till they got quite tired, he standing in the midst the while, as quiet

---

ministers were denied higher education. By the late Seventeenth Centure, funds were set up to establish colleges. Two were set up later at Bristol and Stepney. Stepney College became Regent's Park College, later part of the University of London. It opened in 1811 with William Newman as its first principal. [*From Stepney to St. Giles : the story of Regent's Park College, 1810-1960* / R.E. Cooper. – London : Carey Kingsgate, 1960.]

and good-humoured as he could make himself. At length they got tired and let him go, and he went to his own company.

The other young gentleman I referred to was the son of a gentleman farmer, Mr. Price of Llwyrgbrain. Mr. John Price was a man of superior intellectual endowments, and was soon called upon by the church to exercise his abilities in the work of the ministry. Although he had had a liberal education, still he thought it desirable to become more acquainted with the Classical languages, and having spent some time with a private tutor in Shrewsbury, he accepted a loving and cordial invitation to preside over the church of which he was a member.

An effort was made to build a chapel, and one was soon erected on Newtown green. The dear young pastor entered upon the great work full of delightful anticipations. His whole soul was in his Master's work. Lovely, and greatly beloved by all who knew him, he became a great blessing to the church, the town, and the country for many miles around.

It appeared as if God raised up this young gentleman on purpose to allay the horrible opposition to religion which had always existed in the hearts of the people throughout the whole of this neighbourhood, and it answered the purpose to admiration.

But God who gave this great blessing, did, in a few years, withdraw it, by calling the lovely young pastor to the skies, as if too good for earth. He died in youth when the dew was fresh upon him, and at a period when he was remarkably useful. Devout men carried him to his burial, and made great lamentation over him.

This was to the church a mysterious and trying dispensation. Yet the Lord was kind to the people, and sent them a successor worthy of the dear man whom he had so recently called away. The successor was the Rev⁴ John Jones, a member of the Baptist Church at Dolea, under the pastorate of the Rev⁴ D. Evans, who had, with other young men, spent some time under the Rev⁴ Kilpin, at Kidderminster. A good man and fully competent for the office of tutor.

Mr. Jones possessed many special accomplishments. Nature had done its part for him. He was tall and comely in person, well-proportioned, full six feet high, with a bright eye, a cheerful countenance, a fine musical voice, a warm heart, and an eloquent tongue. He was master of both languages in which he was accustomed to preach. When he spoke in the Welsh language a Welshman who had never heard him before might suppose that he knew nothing of the English tongue, and when he spoke in English an Englishman might conclude that he knew nothing of the Welsh. His moral powers were of the first order. So good, so feeling for all in trouble, travailing in birth for souls, and God gave him many souls for his hire, and seals to his ministry.

The congregations and the church increased much under his ministry, and the chapel, with its three galleries, was not large enough to accommodate the crowds which attended his ministry. The place must be enlarged. We went to work; the house was finished, large, capable of seating about 800[10] persons.

The day of opening dawned, and all the town was on tip-toe expectation. Great and popular ministers came in from England. In due time the Revd Isaiah Birl of Birmingham ascended the pulpit and read a short text.

"All hail." I remember a few introductory remarks. This was the Redeemer's salutation on meeting his sorrowing disciples after his resurrection from the dead. He had come from heaven to earth to prepare himself for the great battle. He had entered the dread territory of the allied forces of earth and hell. He had crushed the old serpent's head, and broken down all the powers of darkness. "I have taken out the sting of death, the bars of the grave I have torn up and they can never be replaced again. I have all your conquered foes under bolts and locks, and here are all the keys safe at my girdle. All hail."

"Friends", said the preacher, looking around, "I am come to congratulate you. You have enlarged your tent. You have lengthened your cords, and strengthened your stakes, hence this fine imposing building. I say to you, all hail." Why it was like an electric shock.

The Revd Jenkin Thomas, of Oxford, next ascended the pulpit with some difficulty. The place was so packed that he had to walk over, or on the backs of the pews. He read his text.

---

[10] "1500" written over original "800".

"May the Lord God of your fathers make you a thousand times as many more as ye are, and bless you as he hath promised."

Here I must stop. I cannot describe it; the flood of eloquence, the thunder of his oratory and the pungency of his appeals were surprising. We were almost transported with delight. We heard Mr. Thomas preach again in the afternoon and evening with increased pleasure, if possible. The crowds in attendance each time were immense. He was asked to give us another sermon at six o'clock next morning, but did not give his full consent till after ten o'clock at night. Some half dozen of us went in search of the old bellman, but he was gone to bed, in a state not to be described. However, the wife said that she would let us have the bell if we could get any one to go round with it. We thought of an old militia-man, a member of our church, who might not mind doing the thing. We went to his house, but to our surprise and mortification we met with a refusal, and gave no small offence to his good wife for entertaining such low thoughts of her husband. One of our number was asked, but, no, he retreated back from the bell several paces.

"Then," said I, " give me the bell." I rang it out and cried with a loud voice. "Please to take notice. The Revd Jenkin Thomas of Oxford will preach at the Baptist Chapel tomorrow morning at six o'clock. God save the King." I went to all the old bellman's halting places to proclaim the good news. Great numbers of people followed me. I became so popular that several persons wished to share my honours by having a ring or two, but, no thank you, I kept them all to myself. It was a good thing for me that the children of the town were safe in their beds, or I should have had the streets filled with laughing faces and noisy tongues.

The Chapel, large as it was, was nearly filled at that early hour, and many a kind nod, and approving smile the good people gave me as they walked up the aisles. We had another rich treat.

The feast of reason and the flow of soul. When I first became united with these good people I found that many of them, like myself, felt very desirous to be useful, the young people especially. The Sunday School was then in a very low state. We went to work, and in the first year we raised this school from forty, in round numbers, to two hundred. The next year from two hundred to four hundred. The third year we had no less than six hundred children. This success told so well upon other congregations in the town that after a time scarcely a child was found playing in the streets or fields on the Sabbath day. We had, for a time, what may be called a press gang; two persons from each congregation went continually about in search of naughty boys and girls, gathering them into one or the other of these schools as their parents might choose. The change for good in the place became truly marvellous. I ought to share this interesting fact, that my worthy friend, Mr. Samuel Morgan, was chosen as the first superintendent of this school, and the good gentleman occupied that honourable post for about thirty years.

I have often thought that few ministers have, in their day, turned more young people to righteousness than my much respected and worthy friend, Mr. Morgan, had done.

My mind was, about this time, much exercised respecting the work of the ministry. I kept the thing to myself. I really thought it presumption for me ever to think of such a thing. Some people, now and then, on hearing me address the Sunday School, said they were sure I had abilities to preach the Gospel. I went with two very judicious old members of the church to a village station one Sabbath and, on the road, they urged me to preach to the people. I, at length, agreed to try. I did so in the best way I could and pleased the people very much. I preached on two or three other occasions, with much fear and anxiety lest I was running unsent by the great Master himself.

Tidings came to the ears of the Church, at our Jerusalem, that I taught the people without the sanction of the Church, and that my conduct ought to be enquired into. A venerable man, one of the deacons, came up to me in the street one Tuesday and said, "Mr. Breeze, our worthy pastor and the deacons wish to hear you preach. We have often talked about you as a man likely to be useful in the ministry, and hearing of your late attempts to speak, I have been requested to ask you to preach before the church tomorrow evening at seven o'clock; that we may either encourage you, or think no more about you." This was the good Mr. Joseph Davis to perfection, blunt and very kind-hearted. I was present according to order, but in a very disturbed state of mind. Having to conduct all the service myself, I gave out the first hymn.

> O my soul what means this sadness?
> Wherefore art thou thus cast down?
> Let thy griefs be turned to gladness;
> Bid, each anxious fear be gone.
> Look to Jesus
> And rejoice in his dear name.

I really trembled much through nervousness, but did the best I could, and I did look to Jesus, I believe, if ever I did; and have the impression that he did help me.

It was customary for young men to appear before the church three times but, as a preacher was wanted for the afternoon of the next Sabbath in the chapel, I was requested to take that service, and had the hearty approval of all the church without any further probation. From this time my preaching engagements became very numerous. I received applications from all quarters; and was engaged every Sabbath somewhere or other, far and near.

My dear Pastor often talked to me seriously, and encouragingly, about my going to college in order to be educated for the work of the ministry. He soon afterwards consulted the Rev^d Mr. Thomas, President of the College at Abergavenny, upon the subject, but he could not hold out any hope upon the subject at present, nor for several years to come. The applications had been very numerous, and it was their rule, in order to avoid partiality, to receive the candidates according to the date of application. My turn, if I applied then, would come in about four years.

This being the case, I gave up all hopes of going to college, and began to lay down my plans for commencing business as a flannel manufacturer. I found that there was a small factory on the Newtown Green to let. I applied for it, and was so fortunate to secure it. It was just the thing for a beginner, being small. I began to make preparations. I ordered a spinning wheel and a couple of looms of a young man who was about beginning business as a machine maker, and, as he was in want of timber, I advanced him some cash, to enable him to make a start. I also had somewhat hastily procured goods to go up to London, supposing it would be to my advantage to renew my acquaintance with the London drapers.

I arrived safely at the great city, and took up my quarters in Cecil Court, St. Martin's Lane. The good people at whose house I stayed were quite respectable, so that I felt at home with them during my stay. It was soon found out in the great city that I had been accustomed to preach; so it led to frequent engagements. I preached several times for my relative, the Revd E. Lewis of Highgate, and for others also. I was invited to go one Monday to the Baptist monthly meeting, Devonshire Square, and went into the vestry after the morning service to dine with the ministers and friends.

I was introduced by the worthy Pastor of the church, the Revd Timothy Thomas, a true lover of his country and countrymen. He kindly introduced me as Mr. Breeze from Wales. The sound of the name produced a wonderful effect, and several asked me if I was related to the late celebrated Samuel Breeze, and on my replying that I was, several of them greeted me with kind smiles, and a warm shake of the hand.

At the dinner table I sat by the side of a grave, sedate-looking personage, and he asked me over what church in the principality I was pastor.

"Sir," I replied, "I am no pastor, only a humble village preacher."

"Doctor," said a minister for whom I had preached, "Mr. Breeze ought to be a pastor."

"If so," said the Doctor to me, "how is it that you have not become a pastor?"

To this I replied that we had but one college in Wales, and that my pastor had kindly applied to that College for me without success.

"Well," said he, "I have no doubt you can get in at Stepney if you apply."

I looked up at him with some interest, saying, "do you think so, Sir?"

A minister, overhearing the conversation said to me, "Mr. Breeze, you are speaking to Dr. Newman, the President of Stepney College."

I tried to make an apology to the good man, but he would not hear it.

"Say not a word", said he, "here is my address. Come to my house on Wednesday next without fail. Take a cup of tea with me at 4 o'clock and preach to my people at Bow that evening."

There was no saying nay to this invitation. I went, and found the gentleman at home. He received me kindly and asked me several questions. I ventured to ask him many questions also, but found him very cautious in his replies. We went off to the Chapel. There were present in a good-sized vestry some fifty or sixty persons.

"You conduct the service, Mr. Breeze", said the Doctor, "and I will conclude by prayer."

I entered the little rostrum with no envious feelings, but tried to look up to my great Friend and I believe he helped as I went through the service with tolerable comfort. He concluded by prayer; from which I could clearly learn what he thought of me, then, walking up to me warmly thanked me for my services.

"God has evidently given you abilities for the ministry, Mr. Breeze, and it becomes you to cultivate and improve them. You will have to give up all thought of secular business, and devote yourself entirely to God. You have my most cordial patronage. Write without delay to your pastor, to the church of which you are a member, and to any ministers in Wales, or in London, who may have heard you, for testimonials &c. When you have received them bring them to the College, on any day about one o'clock." He and Mrs. Newman would go with me to the coach office, to see me safely off. God helped me through this difficulty. How wonderful and mysterious are his ways.

I wrote to the different parties for my credentials. They were promptly sent and very kindly written. I took them to Stepney, a good handful of them. I was introduced to the good Doctor, and to the Rev^d Mr. Young, the classical tutor. They received me kindly, and examined my recommendations. When they had read them through, they both said, "very satisfactory indeed, highly so." I was then asked how long I had been a Christian; and what were the means whereby I was brought to the knowledge of the truth, with more questions of that kind, to which I briefly replied; and in doing so my feelings were moved even to tears. The good men caught the sympathy, so we three wept together.

The Doctor saw a friend of mine a few days after. I preached for him, and he said, "Mr. L__, I was very much pleased with your young friend Mr. Breeze, and it appears to me that he only wants what we have to give. Polish, to make him a very useful and respectable minister of the Gospel. I will do what I can to promote the object which he has in view."

To a minister of Wales, he said, "Mr. Breeze is as well as admitted." The minister told this to my friends in Newtown in passing through, so that they knew the secret of my success before I did myself.

I asked the gentlemen how long it would be before I should have to appear before the Committee of the College; and was informed that they would meet on the 26th of this month, March, so I had to wait in town till the time came.

The day at length arrived, and on calling at the Baptist Mission House, I found there three candidates for admission into the College besides myself. We four felt nervous and anxious.

Mr. Jones, a young man from Cardigan, was first called. He soon came back and said, rather cheerfully, "admitted." He, some years afterwards, became President of Stepney College.

Mr. Caldicott, Northamptonshire, was the second man called. Now Doctor Caldicott, Montreal, Canada.[11] He returned admitted.

"Mr. Breeze, Newtown," was called next. The sound of my name actually made me jump. I walked into the room. There were the dread committee sure enough. The large room was well-seated round by a body of as fine, venerable men as I ever saw, and they appeared to be so really good that I lost my fears all at once. Why, they looked more like living fathers than stern judges. Doctor Newman stood up and said in a grave manner,

"Mr. Breeze, please to stand up behind that table. Read any text you like out of that pocket Bible and give us a few thoughts in the briefest way you can."

I read a text, and spoke for about five minutes, when the Doctor lifted up his hand, "Please to retire into the next room, and we will consider your case." I did so, and had scarcely turned myself round when I was recalled. The Doctor said kindly,

"Mr. Breeze, I am happy to tell you that you are admitted. Leave your address with Mr. Cramp, the Secretary, and you will soon hear from us." I bowed my thanks and walked out.

In coming out I met the fourth candidate, Mr. James Flood from Salisbury. He also was admitted. I afterwards became very much attached to my good brother Flood, a man who lived very near to God, and became very useful in the Church. After he left College he spent about 18 months as pastor of the Baptist Church at Kislingbury, Northamptonshire, from which place he went as a missionary to Jamaica. By God's help he did a good work, and was very much beloved till his health failed him, when he had to return to England. He afterwards took the pastorate of the Baptist Church at Melbourne, Cambridgeshire, where he proved a great blessing.

I received, a few days after my admission, the following letter from the Revd J. M. Cramp, Secretary to the College:

March, 1823

Dear Sir;

I have received a letter from the Revd W. Gray, informing me that he can receive you immediately. You will therefore have the goodness to repair to him as soon as possible, that no time may be lost. May a blessing attend your engagements with him.

To this end you must be diligent, circumspect, humble and watchful. You are aware that Mr. Gray lives at Chipping Norton, Oxfordshire. Go as soon as you can.

Yours &c.
J. M. Cramp

Chapel Place
Southwark.

I hastened home, settled all my affairs, and preached in the great Chapel once on the Sabbath, a kind of farewell sermon. The first hymn I gave out was the following. It was read with feeling by myself, and I saw that the great congregation felt it as much as the young preacher.

Mysteries of Divine Providence

Cowper

God moves in a mysterious way
His wonders to perform
He plants his footsteps in the sea
And rides upon the storm.

Deep in unfathomable mines
Of never failing skill
He treasures up his bright designs
And works his sovereign will.

Ye fearful saints fresh courage take;
The clouds ye so much dread
Are big with mercyes and shall break
In blessing on your head.

Judge not the Lord by feeble sense
But trust him for his grace;
Behind a frowning providence
He hides a smiling face.

His purposes will ripen fast
Unfolding every hour;
The bud may have a bitter taste
But sweet will be the flower.

6

THE YOUNG STUDENT BEGINS HIS STUDIES

To DESCRIBE THE last parting scenes might not be wise in me. It might savour of vanity or egotism. Suffice it to say that I mounted the old coach and left the town, amid the smiles, blessings, and waving of hands of the crowds who came to see me off. Hundreds of my dear old friends are now in heaven. May the Lord keep watch over their ashes and prepare me and the dear aged ones still remaining in the valley below to ascend the holy Mount above, again to meet those whom we loved so much on earth, to be as happy, and as bright, as they now are.

I arrived safely at Chipping Norton, and was very kindly received by Mr. and Mrs. Gray and the students.

We were soon found in class together, four of us; Mr. Wake, Mr. Flood, Mr. Breeze, Mr. Caldicott, and, after a little time, Mr. Garner was added to our number. All Stepney men.

Captain Price of Llwn-y-Brain, and his excellent sister, had kindly given me some of their late worthy brother's classical books, which I found very useful. They gave me also *50 Manuscript Sermons* which I highly prize for their neatness and truthfulness, quite model sermons, short, and full of evangelical matter.

We who were last admitted were started in Latin and Greek. We had, each one, to give in weekly the outlines of a sermon; alternate months a sermon, an essay and very much beside, the more the better. We thought it a great privilege to be there, and felt very wishful to improve the precious hours.

The first vacation came upon us rather suddenly. I had received two invitations to supply during the holidays. The first was from the Independent Church at Deddington, which my tutor said was a great compliment passed upon me. The second came from a home missionary whose station was in the neighbourhood. Mr. Gray wished me to take the latter, as he should want me to supply for him a Sabbath or two during that time. When we had been dismissed I went to Little Tew, a central village to those I had to supply. Board and lodging had been provided for me at the comfortable home of two good old people in easy circumstances, where I found myself pretty much at home. I had to supply this village, another called Cleaveley, and a third of the name of Swerford. There were many, very good people in those villages, and I became a wonderful favourite with all the people, as a new man generally is, for a time at least.

The places became much crowded, and several souls were converted to God. Of this, I have no doubt whatever.

Friend Carter, a labourer, and his good wife, were a very worthy couple. I have spent many profitable hours on their clean hearth, and before their bright little fire. They had their cottage comforts and no mistake. He was a hard labourer, and honest man, and, with the carefulness of his industrious wife, always contrived to pay twelve pence to the shilling. It had not always been the case with them. They had lived for years like too many of their neighbours, without God, and without hope in the world. The wife went to hear the Gospel one Sabbath, and received a blessing. She was brought to love the Saviour and wished to follow him in his ordinances.

One day she said to her husband, "John, I am going to Chipping Norton next Sabbath, to be baptized by Mr. Gray, and I want you to go with me." He started with surprise, looked very savage, and swore that if she went he would kill her. At all events he would never live with her any more, that was certain.

The poor woman looked at him kindly, and said, "My dear John, I must go, and let me beg of you not to hinder me."

"I tell you what," said he, "I will keep to my word," and then went out of the house in a great passion.

The next Sabbath morning came. The good woman was up early, got the breakfast all ready, but it was eaten in silence, for each was afraid to speak. She put on her bonnet, and kindly smiled, saying, "Good morning, my dear," and started off, not knowing whether she should ever see the inside of her little cottage again. He soon started off, and went some ten miles to see his parents, and to tell them his troubles. He assured them that he never would live with his wife again.

"I tell thee what," said the father, "I would go back to her, and I would give her as good a thrashing as any disobedient wife ever had."

"Yes, John," said the old mother, "give her a good one, for she deserves it."

John returned for home after a while, resolved to turn wicked advice to some practical account. Wending his way homeward with a heavy step and an aching heart, feeling vexed with his wife and angry with himself, he came to a pool of water, and a wicked thought came suddenly into his mind, that he had better get rid of his sorrows all at once by drowning himself in that water. He turned down the bank and was going into the pool when a better thought came to his help, and through mercy, saved him from self-destruction. It was somewhat like as if a person spoke to him these words,

"Now you are going to follow the devil into the water to be drowned, while your wife has been following Jesus Christ into the water to be saved." He burst into tears and went home a wiser man. His wife received him with affectionate smiles.

"My dear wife," said he, most deeply affected, "will you forgive me?" Imagine the rest, only let me say, that before many months had passed, friend Carter had the pleasure of following his blessed Lord through the baptismal waters, to the no small joy of his dear wife.

Just before I came to this village I heard of the death of my dear and ever to be beloved mother[1]. Before I left home we had parted at a throne of grace, with a firm belief that our next meeting would be at a throne of glory, and I continue to believe it still. I hear that she died in a happy frame of mind, singing her favourite hymn as long as she had strength

---

[1] Susanna Brees, of Clogau, was buried at Llanwnnog on 17 May 1823, aged 65.

to articulate. At length she sweetly fell asleep in Jesus, and her spirit was conveyed to the happy world where the blessed Saviour dwells.

The words of the hymn are as follows:

Death Anticipated in Faith and Hope
Ryland

Ah! I shall soon be dying
Time swiftly glides away
But on my Lord relying
I hail the happy day.
The day when I must enter
Upon a world unknown;
My helpless soul I venture
To Jesus Christ alone.

He once a spotless victim
Upon Mount Calvary bled;
Jehovah did afflict him,
And bruise him in my stead.
Hence all my hope arises
Unworthy as I am;
My soul most dearly prizes
The sin-atoning Lamb

It was an open funeral, as is the good custom in Wales. Some 300 people attended, and a religious service was held.

AT THE CLOSE of this first summer's vacation we met again at our beloved home, the house of our esteemed tutor; and right glad we were, as we students felt a strong attachment towards each other, and, happily, it gained strength, if possible, even to the last. We had in common a strong fellow-sympathy and affectionate feeling for each other. We loved Jesus Christ. We were engaged in his holy service. We studied together, sang and prayed together, and we did, generally, live together in strong Christian affection. Day by day we found our employment hard, dry work, but, on the whole, pleasant and profitable. Our Sabbaths were delightful, vacations on a small scale. We were generally engaged preaching the gospel in the villages near or in supplying the churches in the towns around when our help was required. We found the good people invariably kind wherever we went, and the more so as we came to know more of each other. I may say that all of them were glad to receive Mr. Gray's students into their houses, and into their pulpits. Why we should have been stupids and not students if we did not feel comfortable and thankful in the midst of so much that was cheering. Besides we found Mr. and Mrs. Gray acted the part of parents towards us, and the young people [were] as kind and affectionate as young people could be. Thus between engagements and comforts we found ourselves at the beginning of the next summer vacation.

I had received and accepted an invitation to preach at Woodstock for the next vacation, on condition that I take to myself two weeks to visit my beloved relatives and friends at Newtown.

As soon as I was set at liberty, I started off for home, sweet home, where I was kindly welcomed by my old friends, among whom I spent two weeks, which seemed to me but as two days.

This is a changing world, full of *adieus* and 'farewells'. I will not at present stay to recount the parting with my friends, who were evidently as warmhearted as ever, for my right hand brought away unmistaken proofs of the warm pressure of their friendship. The skin literally scaled off from all the middle joints of the fingers.

I arrived safely at Woodstock, that once royal city, where many a dark and cruel deed has been perpetrated.[2] Who could help thinking of Henry the Second, and of Eleanor his Queen, who was driven by jealousy, and a

---

[2] Woodstock was the seat of English monarchs for several centuries. It was called Woodstow, "the woody place". Alfred the Great translated Boethius here. Here Henry I built the first enclosed park in England. Elizabeth was imprisoned at Woodstock by Mary. Queen Anne granted the manor to John Churchill. £500,000 was voted by parliament for building Blenheim palace. Woodstock became famous for its leather gloves. The trade declined, but still employed about a thousand people in 1863. *Dutton, Allen's Directory of Berkshire, Buckinghamshire and Oxfordshire, 1863.*

just indignation, to remove one so fair to an early grave; marked out only by a humble tomb inscribed with lines so true.

> The tomb does here enclose
> The world's most beauteous rose, etc.

Posterity feels thankful to King John for raising this tomb to her memory, nor do we feel regret that some years afterwards, a retributive providence brought up the royal seducer barefooted to receive a sharp flagellation at the tomb of Thomas à Becket. God will not let the wicked always go unpunished.

This magnificent palace, this spacious park, and these beautiful gardens are sadly marred when you think of Fair Rosamond's Bower, the poisoned cup, and the faded Beauty. What a dark shade to hang over a place that ought to be a paradise, and to have its past associated with all that is virtuous and morally excellent.

When I came to Woodstock, I met with a cordial welcome from the good people who looked for my coming. It was not my first visit, so that we were not strangers to each other. There were some good souls in the town then and, since that time, the number has doubtless increased. It even then presented a pleasing contrast to the state of things some years before, when the late Venerable, the Revd James Hinton of Oxford, and one of his worthy deacons, Mr. Bartlett, while attempting to hold a religious service in the town, were assailed by the mob, and very narrowly escaped with their lives, being sadly bruised and ill-treated by the maddened and furious ruffians. It is worthy of remark, that one of the worst of these fellows was, in my time, a doorkeeper of our sanctuary, and a consistent member of the church. I venture to say that he never forgave himself for this his act of cruelty to his dying day. I have often seen him shed tears when the painful circumstance has been narrated.

The attendance at the chapel was very good and several persons were brought to the knowledge of the truth. The circumstances of the people were generally good, as there was carried on considerable business in the town in the manufacture of gloves. For who has not heard of the

Woodstock gloves?

I had to preach on a week evening at a village some two miles off, called Wootton, where the good people had been much vexed by some mischievous young fellows of the place, who came to disturb them when assembled together for divine worship. Sometimes they would beat the door, break a pane in the windows, or contrive to let stones down through the chimney, which was really very dangerous. One night they blew some asafoetida[3] through the key hole, which set the people all a-coughing, and they were obliged to run out into the fresh air as fast as they could.

Now I suppose that the young fellows did these tricks merely for the sake of fun, to have something to laugh about, and not for any particular hatred to religion. However, my friends said to me that a few of them would go over with me; and some ten or twelve persons went one evening and no sooner had we met in the house than my friends saw the leader of these naughty disturbers walk in, and they expected, of course, that we should have some trouble, and kept their eyes upon him to watch his movements. They saw the young man very attentive to what was said, then the tears flowed freely, and shortly after the man cried out aloud for mercy, and begged us to pray to God for him, and two or three of us prayed for him expressly. There was no stopping of his tears. It was many weeks before he could believe in Christ and obtain peace of mind. At length the blessing came, and he became as happy as he had been miserable before. I saw the wisdom of God in giving me soul troubles at the time of my conversion, by this and other circumstances, that I might know how to comfort others in their sorrows. I afterward found out that a sister of this young man had been converted under a sermon of mine at Woodstock some time before, so I expect she advised her brother to come and hear me.

The vacation being over, the good people parted with me very reluctantly and I half wished in my own mind to have stayed longer, but the stern rule of duty forbad me that pleasure. We again met at our good home and found it pleasant to do so. We were allowed a few days to talk over our

---

[3] An acrid gum resin with a strong smell like that of garlic, obtained from certain Asian plants of the umbelliferous genus Ferul, and used in condiments [From *Canadian Oxford Dictionary*, 1998 ed.]

adventures, and to visit our kind friends in the town, for we always had more invitations than we could possibly attend to.

We resumed our studies in the best way we could, and did, I think, feel conscientious in the matter; as we felt that we ought to make progress for the credit of our worthy tutor, and in justice to ourselves, as well as to meet the wishes of our kind patrons. The ministers who called upon Mr. Gray generally paid us a short visit, and spoke kindly to the sons of the prophets.

One day an eminent minister called, and wished to know if I was related to the late Samuel Breeze, and if I had ever heard Christmas Evans. He said he had heard them both at Bristol several times, and that he had never heard such extraordinary men in his life. "If," said he, "two angels had ever become incarnate, and lived here on earth, it was in the persons of Samuel Breeze and Christmas Evans."

We continued to go out on the Sabbath as formerly, and, as far as we could judge our own spirits, we felt a great pleasure in the work.

The third summer vacation arrived, like many things which come to persons hard at work, almost before we looked for it.

I had accepted a kind invitation from Mr. Jean, the pastor of the Baptist Church at Campden, for the vacation, as he wished to go out for a time. I found this church in a very healthy and lively state. There were many young people who were members of the church, a large Sunday School, and the congregation filled the large chapel well. I was reminded a little of the cheerful state of things at Newtown. I found that I must exert all my powers to keep things together during the absence of my good brother. I believe my visit was blessed for good as I had the pleasure of hearing from the people, and from the pastor himself, on his return home. At a farewell meeting, he passed a vote of thanks for my very acceptable service &c.

Quite unexpectedly we were rather suddenly called to pass through a great change. Our good tutor had supplied the Baptist Church at College Street, Northampton, and had received an unanimous and pressing invitation to the pastorate there, which he felt it his duty to accept. He told me that the president wished me to go up to Stepney College for twelve months or so, but that he should like me and Mr. Flood to settle near him in Northamptonshire, and that he could get us invitations to that effect. We talked the matter over. We saw, if we went to Stepney, we should have to be juniors for our year, and as juniors are not sent out to preach the first year, we thought we should not like it. On the other hand, as we had spent three long summer vacations as a sort of temporary pastors, besides our long practice in preaching whereby we had gained considerable experience, we had better go into the work as soon as we might have a call in providence to do so. We told Mr. Gray our decision, and he took our several cases into consideration.

The Lord did soon open a way for us all, and the social and friendly fraternity was soon broken up.

We felt it much. Mr. and Mrs. Gray felt it, although they had much to occupy their attention. I think the good people in the town, in the villages around, the ministers and churches in the neighbourhood, felt it as much as ourselves. They said that Messrs. Murrell, Philips, Phelpp, Elliott and Dorney had left, now the Rev^d. W. Gray, Messrs Wake, Flood, Caldicott, Breeze and Garner are going also. What shall we do without them.

Well it was a great loss to the various localities we had been accustomed to visit, of this there can be no doubt; a loss which they have not made up to this day.

My promised invitation came. It was from West Haddon, and I addressed myself for the journey. I took friendly farewell, and with my carpet bag and umbrella, quite equal to Jacob, his was a staff only[4], also to the great Teacher—Foxes have holes, &c.[5], I mounted the coach, and rode to the nearest town, and most likely walked the rest of the distance, or, perhaps had the chance of a ride. I really do not remember now, but this I recollect well, that I reached the village, and was very kindly received by the people at the house where it was arranged for me to take up my quarters. It

---

[4] Jacob left Beersheba in Canaan after he had tricked Isaac out of the blessing meant for Esau. Esau was threatening to kill Jacob. There is no mention of a staff in this account. *[Genesis 27-28, New English Bible]*

[5] "Jesus replied, 'Foxes have their holes, the birds their roosts; but the Son of Man has nowhere to lay his head.' Another man, one of his disciples, said to him, 'Lord, let me go and bury my father first.' Jesus replied, 'Follow me, and leave the dead to bury their dead.'" *[Matthew 8:20-22, and, similarly, Luke 9:58-60, NEB]*

was with an old gentleman, and his two daughters, a very comfortable sort of people, and the accommodation all that I could desire. I heard a poor account of the state of things at the Chapel; that there had been a division in the church, through the late pastor leaving; that there were now two parties, and that there was no pleasing them. They had tried several ministers, and very good ones too, but if one party liked one, the other did not; as if each determined to oppose the other, merely for the sake of the thing. "Well," thought I, "if this is the case I am in for it," and I thought I would wait a little, and not jump at any hasty conclusions. If the worst came, I would pick up my carpet bag again, and go up right to Stepney College, as I felt sure the good Doctor would receive me.

Sabbath morning came, and at the proper time I went up to the chapel, a good-sized building, and quite a respectable congregation. I had a good service, and the people were very attentive, and evidently pleased. In coming out, several stayed to speak to me, and seemed glad of the opportunity to do so. I was told before the evening service that the two parties had become one, and all were loud in praise of the young Welshman. They ventured already to say that Mr. Breeze was just the preacher they wanted. The Chapel was well filled in the evening, unusually so, as I was afterwards informed; and I felt as if I were at home with the good people already. The rich and the poor alike were pressing in their invitations. It was a new thing to them, as matters had been of late, but the better sort of them said that God had answered prayer.

I could look about me a little on the morrow. I found Haddon to be a pretty village, situated on a hill or rising ground, and very clean, as there was a good fall for the water. It had a Church, a Wesleyan and a Baptist Chapel in it, with a population of about 1600 persons, situated on the high road from Northampton to Rugby and 77 miles from London.

There are several respectable houses in the parish, and well-to-do families, some of them more than well-to-do, really wealthy, and the Baptist Chapel comes in for some of these. So far, so good. May God give them the true honours.

The Gospel has done much for this favoured country. It has been, at times, my opinion that the Northamptonshire Christians were the most kind-hearted people I ever saw since I left Wales. The Chapels and Dissenters are numerous and useful wherever you go. It is in the meantime a pleasing fact that where the Gospel is faithfully preached in the Episcopal Church you meet with Christians of a similar type. May their number and purity increase.

The large towns have many chapels in them, nor is there a village of any size but has one or two, and a stated ministry in it. I had not to go far to seek the society of a brother minister and Christian friends. My esteemed tutor, the Revd W. Gray continued his friendship very cordially; and his congregation treated me with marked respect and Christian courtesy, most likely on the ground of the friendship that existed between their beloved pastor and myself.

The good man was deservedly popular among his people, and also very useful. This good feeling continued for many years. I preached for him one Sabbath, soon after I came to West Haddon, and was delighted to see the crowded congregations. Every available space in the large chapel was occupied, so that I got with difficulty into the pulpit between the people seated on the steps of the stairs. This was constantly the case from Sabbath to Sabbath.

This congregation has been highly favoured for many years, with some of the ablest of ministers and best of men. May many blessings rest on the present talented pastor, and may his days be long and useful.

My probation month terminating at West Haddon I received a very cordial invitation to the pastorate of the church and the good people were evidently desirous that I should comply with their request, but I urged them to wait for a time, till I should see clearly and satisfactorily what was the will of God in the matter, but that I would continue to supply the pulpit for a time if they had no objections. This they agreed to do. I continued my services for more than fifteen months longer, and then sent in a negative to their kind invitation. This they felt very much indeed, nor did I feel it less.

They had another church meeting, when they agreed unanimously to renew their invitation. This I received, and it perplexed me very much. It was the *vox populi* no doubt, but I could not feel that it was the *Vox Dei*.

I could not see my way clear to stay, and to leave so kind a people against their anxious wishes was the most painful thing of the sort I ever felt, even down to this day. I had my own reasons for adopting this line of conduct, but whether they were just or not was the question that made it so perplexing and painful to me.

The fact was this: I had the impression that very little good had been done by my ministry. I knew that some good had been done and no one complained for want of more prosperity so much as myself. But the sphere of usefulness was so contracted that I felt I had not enough to do by way of Church extension. I had received invitations from other churches, which held out greater prospects of usefulness, and had declined them, and whether I had done right or wrong in these cases I was at a loss to know. While my mind was cogitating these matters over I received an invitation from the Baptist Church, Lechlade, Gloucestershire. I did not think much of it, but made up my mind to go there for a month, to see the place and the people, and I answered the invitation to that effect.

When I told the good people that I should leave them for a month, at least, they really could not understand me, and positively I could not understand myself. Now I can, as I have found out since then that God had very much for me to do in Gloucestershire and Wiltshire. It is not in man that walketh to direct his steps. The last service came, and such another service I should be sorry to see. There was little else but weeping, and broken sentences, and hopes that I would come back again. I said that I really thought I should, and we bade farewell to each other. I did not leave next morning quite as soon as I intended. A little maid, passing by my window, saw that I was not gone and went up the street weeping aloud. Being asked what was the matter, she replied, "Mr. Breeze is not gone." In a few minutes some dozen or fifteen of the friends walked into the rooms, again to say goodbye, when one of them proposed that we should have a short prayer meeting; and we did. Each brother prayed very earnestly that God would bless me, and bring me back again safely. I left them and departed. Yes, left the kindest people I ever knew in all my ministerial engagements. The Revd D. White of Cirencester called upon some of them while visiting his friends in the neighbourhood, and, when informed of the above particulars, seriously questioned the propriety of the step I had taken in leaving a people so respectable, so loving, and so united as they were.

Before I finish my history of this favoured county, I should like to record a few things about its worthy ministers and friends whom I found so fraternal, and shall begin with my good brother, the Revd John Mack of Clipstone.

Mr. Mack was the esteemed Pastor of the Baptist Church in the above village. A Scotchman by birth, he had been a soldier for many years. He was converted to God when in the army, and, for a time, preached the Gospel to groups of the soldiers and anywhere that he had an opportunity to do so. As he became more known he was frequently invited to preach in chapel and his services became highly appreciated. I spent a Sabbath at Deal some years ago where I occupied the pulpit of the Baptist Chapel. The worthy deacon, at whose house I stayed, was high in his praise of Mr. Mack. He informed me that he had been with the regiment at Eyethorn Barracks, and had often preached at their chapel. He said also that when he left with the regiment for Manchester he called in upon him to say goodbye, and to light his short pipe. In this march they had to halt at Leicester for a few days' rest. Mr. Mack called upon the great Robert Hall, and shewed him his credentials. Mr. Hall read them, and warmly taking hold of his hand, said, "Sir, you must preach for me tonight. It is our evening service, Sir, and I will have no denial."

The soldier consented to preach. He could not help himself for the great man was very positive when he set his mind upon a thing. The good soldier preached a most masterly sermon. Mr. Hall was delighted beyond measure and, meeting him as he came out of the pulpit, took hold of his hand, and with a countenance radiant with smiles, said, "You shall not stay in the army, Sir, if money can purchase your release." Mr. Mack replied, "Mr. Hall, I thank you much for your kind expressions, and shall feel thankful to God to become a free man once more."

Mr. Hall soon got up the redemption price, some ninety pounds, I am told, as men were scarce at that time. The regiment had to march before they had time to settle the matter. However he was told that the money could be obtained at a certain Bank at Manchester, after a given date. Mr.

Mack soon after obtained the money and paid down the redemption price, procured a suit of one of the poor fellows, and started off in search of the Rev^d Mr. Birt's Chapel where he had an engagement to preach that evening. He reached the chapel, got in through the vestry, and gave the people a sermon of the first order. Having procured a suit or two of clothes he returned to Leicester, as previously arranged, to wait for further instructions from his friend Mr. Hall.

He was, for the present, introduced to the Baptist Church at Clipstone. Here his ministry was highly appreciated, so that he was soon invited to the pastoral office. He then consulted his good friend Mr. Hall, who advised him strongly to go to Bristol College for a year or two first. Mr. Mack and the church came to an understanding upon the subject, and the good man soon after repaired to Bristol. Mr. Mack was a man of great wit, and cheerful humour. Sometimes, perhaps, he appeared to considerable disadvantage in the eyes of grave and sedate Christians. His playful spirit would, at times, lead persons to accuse him of levity, and the want of due decorum, or ministerial consistency.

It is said of Rowland Hill that he was often grieved and humbled when his almost uncontrollable wit and playful humour would lead him to a betrayal of the Christian character.

I have seen a good deal of brother Mack, and always considered him to be a cheerful Christian, an able minister, a true friend, and possessing the very elements of good nature and social kindness. Anything ludicrous or comical would throw a man of this temperament completely off his guard, or is apt to do so. One evening when at College, in the lecture room, a Welsh student had to preach, and the young man knew but little of the English language. It was cruel to ask him to take his turn with the rest of the students. The subject was the two blind men coming to Christ. He introduced it somewhat in this manner.

"There were two blind mans come to Jesus Christ and Jesus asked them what do you want for me for to do for you. The two blind mans say we want some see, &c."

Now this was too much for Mack, and he actually burst out into a loud laugh in the place. He was very angry with himself, but he felt that he

EBENEZER | *Richard Breeze, Swindon*

could not help himself if there had been a drawn sword before him.

Dr. Ryland felt much vexed about it, and he afterwards called Mack aside, and said to him, "I am sorry you so far forgot yourself in the lecture room. Why you laughed in the presence of the angels."

Mr. Mack replied by proposing this wily question.

"Do you think, Doctor, that the angels would come all the way from heaven to hear Mack preach?" This was too much for the good Doctor, so he walked away, and the matter passed off.

Mr. Mack's society was always very pleasant. His strong memory, his kind heart, and ready wit, were very cheering. All who knew him could not fail to love him. Yet he could be stern when he was a little put out. He was not the man to think that a person must give up his citizenship or his manhood on becoming a Christian, or even a Christian minister. Once at an Association there was a young minister who had tried to introduce the church prayers into his chapel, as a stepping stone to conformity, and that, of course, against the wishes of the people.

"Bates," said Mr. Mack, looking him hard in the face, "they tell me that you have dealings with the Old Lady at Rome and that you are trying to sell her wares without a license." with more to the same effect. The poor fellow felt the deserved castigation, and wept sore. He was a bad young man, and came to a sad end.

Mr. Mack was once at a Baptist missionary meeting in London. He was holding a plate for a collection at one of the doors of Rowland Hill's Chapel, when a young man threw, rather contemptuously, a button on the plate. Mack took him by the collar, with a firm, resolute grasp.

"Sir," said he, "pick up that button." The terrified man was glad enough to do so, in order to get out of the strong vise in which he had so foolishly place himself.

Mr. Mack said to me one day, "Mr. Hall is coming soon to spend a week with me, before he leaves for Bristol. If you come and spend a few days with us I shall be pleased to see you."

I replied that I should be happy to do so, that I should deem it a rich treat.

"Agreed," said he, "and I will let you know the time. I shall invite no one else, that we may have a quiet time of it."

The invitation came, I went over, and certainly had a rich treat. The two great men felt quite at ease; and really after the first hour I felt at home as much as they did.

At another time a gentleman farmer, an uncle of Mrs. Mack's, invited me to spend a few days at his house, in company with Mr. Mack who was about to pay him a visit. I went, and found it good, pleasant, and profitable. The gentleman kindly sent us both home in his carriage. I name this just to say, that some years afterwards the dear man was returning home from visiting the same kind family along the same road. He was overtaken by a heavy fall or rain. When he reached home he was very wet and took a severe cold. From this time he sickened, and died after a short and painful illness. The good man and his great friend, Robert Hall, have long since passed off this mortal stage, and have met each other in the bright world above, where all such kindred spirits meet. If we who still remain may not become so great on earth as they were, yet we may be useful here, and as happy hereafter, for every vessel will be full of joy and love there. What can we desire more?

Some little time before I left West Haddon I went up to London, to spend a week with my relative at Highgate. I preached for him twice. In the evening it was announced that Mr. Breeze would deliver the Missionary Address on the morrow evening at the Independent Chapel. B. Gurney, Esq., residing at the time at Muswell Hill, with his interesting family, attended the chapel, and very kindly invited Mr. Lewis and myself to dinner on the morrow, and to spend the day with Mr. and Mrs. Eustace Carey, who were staying a few weeks with this lovely family, in their beautiful mansion. In the course of the day our conversation turned upon Mr. Hall having recently left for Bristol.

"Oh," said Mr. Carey to me, "you were at Arnsby the other day, and heard Mr. Hall's farewell sermon at the place of his birth previous to his leaving for Bristol."

"Yes, I was, and had the pleasure of seeing you there, Sir."

"Yes," he replied, "what a sublime sermon, such unanswerable arguments." The subject was the resurrection of Christ. "The first preacher was very little compared to him."

"The first preacher," I said, "I have heard many times with great pleasure, but, in my opinion he was little that morning compared with himself. It is said that public men are sometimes themselves, at others above themselves, and sometimes below themselves. I have no doubt that my friend was far below himself that day."

"Well," said he, "there is some truth in that," and he evidently seemed pleased that I had taken the part of an absent friend.

"Besides," I said, "I know of one who said, in going out of the chapel, that the first gentleman was the best preacher. 'As to our Robert,' she said, 'I do not know what he was about. Why he must have thought we all were a number of Sadducees.'"[6]

Mr. Carey laughed outright at this statement, and said,

"I know who it was made that remark. It was old Dame ___ who nursed Mr. Hall when he was a child, and used always to talk so proudly about 'Our Robert'. Well," said he, "Mr. Hall shall hear that tomorrow morning, and will he not be amused?"

Mr. Carey, having heard that I had, some years ago, offered my services to the Baptist Mission to go to Jamaica, urged me now to go to the East Indies, and said that he would arrange matters for me immediately, but I told him that I did not see my way sufficiently clear to take that step at present.

They said that the minister who delivered the address that night two months at the Independent Chapel, made a great blunder. He divided the subject of his address into three parts. He went through "firstly" very well, but when he came to "secondly" his memory failed him, and Mr. said it was so and so, but alas, when he came to "thirdly" it was the same, and the minister of the chapel helped him. They said that they hoped it would not

---

6 It is unclear from the context what Richard Breeze means by this comment. There is no consistent picture of the Sadducees in the Bible. The Jewish historian Josephus describes them as one of the oldest Jewish philosophies. He says that they were influential with a few wealthy families, not with the people, who followed the Pharisees' interpretation of the law. In the New Testament, they are not differentiated from the Pharisees. Both were active in the temple, associated with the priests and opponents of Jesus. [*Harper's Bible Dictionary* / Paul J. Achtemeier ; Society of Biblical Literature. – New York, N.Y., c1985.]

be so this evening. However, we had a good meeting.

Mr. Carey called again about the mission, but I was not in a position to accept an engagement.

> Guide me, O thou Great Jehovah,
> Pilgrim through this barren land.
> I am weak, but thou art mighty,
> Hold me with thy powerful hand.
> Bread of Heaven
> Feed me till I want no more.
>
> Open thou the crystal fountain
> Whence the healing streams do flow.
> Let the fiery cloudy pillar
> Lead me all my journey through
> Strong Deliverer
> Be thou still my strength and shield.
>
> When I tread the verge of Jordan
> Bid my anxious fears subside,
> Guide me through the swelling current
> Land me safe on Canaan's side.
> Songs of praises
> I will ever give to thee.

7

SETTLEMENT AT LECHLADE, GLOUCESTERSHIRE

I CAME TO Lechlade on the 8 February, 1827. Lechlade is a small town in the above county, 74[1] miles from London, having a population of about 1500, and several respectable families. The streets are wide, and the town, I should say, generally healthy, as I have known persons live there to a great age. It is situated on the north bank of the Thames, which is said to be navigable from London down to this place where many boats pass to and fro, and a considerable business is done in coals and other traffick. It has pretty much the appearance of a seaport town, especially in winter, when the floods roll over the banks of the river, and cover the meadows and fields for miles. It appears that Lechlade was a place of considerable importance in the halcyon days of Popery. There are traces of ruins to be seen, which indicate the existence of religious houses, and sacred establishments. Most of the lands in the parish belonged to the church. That it was a place of some resort is evident, as a bridge was erected over the Thames at the expense of the Manor estate, to enable people to come from the other side of the river to attend the church at Lechlade. This was proved some years ago by a long pending law-suit.

Late in the last century the Manor Estate of Lechlade was purchased by the late William Fox, Esq., a retired merchant, a name that ought to be remembered to the end of time, in connexion with Sunday schools.

---

[1] Or 77. The mileage has been rewritten in pencil.

Mr. Raikes of blessed memory, and Mr. Fox[2] were the originators of the greatest of all modern movements, the Sunday School institution, which numbers now, in our own beloved country, some three million children, taught by about 300,000 teachers. Who can tell the future history of this wonderful and very successful undertaking? It is said, on pretty good authority, that Mr. Raikes commenced at first on the system of paid agency, every teacher to be paid for his time and labour in the school. This partially failing, Mr. Fox proposed inviting the young people and others to come to their help as gratuitous teachers. The suggestion told to admiration, and now we have the immense number of voluntary labourers in the Lord's vineyard as stated above. May ten thousand blessings rest upon the efforts of our dear friends in thus endeavouring to impart the knowledge of the Redeemer to the rising generation all over the world, from the rising of the sun to the setting of the same.

> This little seed from heaven
> Shall soon become a tree
> This ever blessed leaven
> Diffused abroad must be
> Till God the Son shall come again
> It must go on, Amen, Amen.

Mr. Fox was a Baptist by profession, and there being no chapel in the town, and the Gospel not preached in the church, he was placed under the necessity of taking his family to the Baptist Chapel at Fairford to wor-

---

[2] "Houses registered for worship in 1784, and 1811, may have been for the Baptists, who under the leadership of William Fox, lord of the manor, built a chapel in Sherborne Street in 1817. The chapel had an evening congregation of 105 in 1851. In 1848 or 1849 a chapel for Congregationalists was built in the Burford road by the Revd. H. J. Crump but his death soon afterwards left it heavily encumbered and, though it had morning and evening congregations of 35 and 80 in 1851, it passed into the hands of the mortgagees and was closed. It was re-opened in 1867 and attempts made to secure it financially but it had closed again by 1888. Shortly before 1888 a Wesleyan chapel was built at the west end of High Street. It and the Baptist chapel remained in use in 1977." William Fox, the founder of the Sunday School Society, bought the manor of Lechlade in 1807. He died in 1826. *[Victoria History of the County of Gloucester, Volume VII. Lechlade, in Brightwells Barrow Hundred]*

ship for several years. At length, feeling his own inconvenience, and the moral destitution of the neighbourhood, he resolved to make an effort to erect a Baptist Chapel in the town. Some of the inhabitants of the place, Dr. Charles Ward and others, sympathised with him in the undertaking. Several of the kind friends at Fairford came to his help. Honoured names that ought not to be forgotten by the lovers of truth; Mr. Jacob Betterton, a man who was always ready, and willing, to help the good cause; Messrs Benjamin and William Thomas, worthy sons of an honoured father, who for many years sustained the office of deacon at the Baptist Chapel with much credit. They were brothers of Mr. John Thomas, one of the first Protestant missionaries to India. This gentleman was articled to the medical profession, and was a member of a Baptist church at Bath. He engaged himself to go as surgeon to a ship going to India. They landed at Calcutta, and the awful state of the poor Heathen Idolaters moved his whole soul in compassion for them. He spoke to some English merchants residing there, upon the subject, and they cordially responded to his feelings, and freely proposed that if he would make an effort to enlighten these poor benighted people, in any way he thought best, they would guarantee his support for a time, while he made the experiment. He named this matter to the Captain of the ship, who kindly released him from his engagement, and then he entered alone and singlehanded upon the great work of saving India.

No small honour to the towns of Fairford and Lechlade to produce two such men, whom God was pleased to employ in two such extraordinary movements, the Sunday School and Christian Missions to the Heathen World.

Mr. Thomas, finding the work too much for one person, bethought himself of seeking help from the churches at home, and from the Baptist churches especially. He left India for London, and when he arrived he found, to his great wonder and delight that some of the Baptist Ministers and churches were actually preparing for the great work of Christian Missions to the heathen; that the Baptist Missionary Society had been formed at Kettering, and that the Rev[d] William Carey was waiting for the Committee to fix on some heathen spot on which he might commence operations. The good man was surprised beyond measure, and saw manifestly the finger of God in it, directing all these things to a happy result. As soon as they could make proper arrangements they set sail for India and the God of Missions went forth with these excellent men, and promoted them to great honour and great usefulness. We at home have been often permitted to read, year after year, with gladdened hearts, the glorious moral achievements wrought by these dear men, and by other men, and women too, of kindred spirits, who subsequently joined them in the mission field.

Baptist Church, Lechlade, built 1817

In returning from this pleasing digression I have to state that the contemplated chapel was built and opened in the year of our Lord 1817, to the great joy of some good people, and to the great regret of others. It so happened that in the summer of the above year there was a considerable drought throughout the whole kingdom for the want of rain, and some of the wise people of Lechlade ascribed that national calamity to that unfortunate chapel, as being the cause of the Divine displeasure, a proof this, in itself, if there were no other, that something of the sort was greatly wanted to teach the inhabitants a better way of thinking and acting.

The chapel being opened, Mr. Fox and his friends secured the services of a minister to supply the pulpit. Mr. Robert Clark, a student from the Baptist College, Bristol, and a member of the Baptist Church, Shortwood, became the first pastor of this infant church, and laboured with considerable success for some eight or ten years, and then removed to Bridgenorth in the county of Salop.

One of the first efforts in connexion with the gospel ministry was the establishment of a Sunday School, which, in the estimation of Mr. Fox was of great importance so that he, his family and friends, entered upon this department of Christian labour with willing minds, and a flourishing Sunday School was the happy result. I shall name one incident in connexion with this school which, I think, ought to be left upon record.

One of the boys attending the school took it into his head to be naughty, stubborn and rebellious, which caused a loud outcry of the teachers against him. They said that the wicked boy must be turned out of the school, or he would discourage all the teachers, and corrupt the other boys.

A kind daughter of Mr. Fox's said, "Let me try him first." The rough and hardened little fellow was brought up to the lady, and he looked defiant, as if he would resist to the last. The lady looked kindly at him and said, "Come, my dear little boy let me hear your lesson." These sweet smiles and kind words cut down deep into the lad's heart, so that he could scarcely refrain from tears.

"Oh," she said, "your lesson is about King David, I see. Now read it through first, and then we will talk about it." The chapter was read through.

"Do you understand it, David? You see the King's name was David, and is not that your name?"

"Yes," replied the boy.

"The king was once a shepherd, and are not you a shepherd?"

"Yes," said the boy.

"Now," said the lady, smiling right in his face, "should you like to be a king?"

"Yes," said the boy, and laughed.

"Well, you may be a king, David, though not in the sense in which David was, yet good boys may become kings and priests unto God. You, David, may have a throne in heaven, royal robes, and a crown of gold on your head. You may become greater than all the kings of this world, &c."

She said much more to the same effect. The lad was overcome, and never did he forget this lesson. Soon after I came to Lechlade these good impressions were deepened under my ministry, and I had the pleasure afterwards of baptizing this young man, of receiving him into the church, of introducing him into the ministry, of recommending him to Horton College, Bradford. Mr. Boyce, for that was his name, went through his studies creditably, and was afterwards settled Pastor over the Baptist Church, New Malton, Yorkshire. He was a warmhearted young man, very energetic, and, at times, truly eloquent. Unusual success attended his ministry at Malton, so that, the first year, 115 persons were received into the church by baptism. Success, more or less, accompanied his labours for the next year or two; but he was tempted to leave this place, where his labours had been so signally blessed, to go to Wakefield, where the people thought they stood in need of a revival also. He went there, and was made very useful. The congregations increased, a new chapel was erected which called forth great labour, and the day of opening came. It was a day of crowds, and of great excitement. The young minister was seized with fits of epilepsy in the evening, of which he never really recovered. He lived a few years after this, but became gradually worse from time to time, and at last died in an asylum, a distressing and mysterious providence. I felt it very much.

This reminds me of a case I saw lately in the *Christian World* Newspaper, not so painful, it is true, but equally instructive. In a large Sunday school in Lancashire, one of the boys became very unruly, quite unmanageable, and must be expelled from the school. This was the verdict passed upon him by some of the teachers. At the close of the school the naughty culprit was brought up to the Superintendent. Here he stood, cared for no one, as hard as a flint, seemed to defy teachers, school and all. Some three hundred boys standing up was rather an imposing sight.

"Now, boys," said the Superintendent, "shall we turn James Kershaw out of the school? If you think it best lift up your right hands."

Not a boy lifted up the hand. Several wept.

"Now, my lads, those of you who are willing for this lad to continue a few Sabbaths more in the school, to see if he will get better, signify it by holding up your right hands."

Up rose a whole forest of hands and smiling countenances. The boy looked on and burst into tears. He was overcome by kindness, and from that moment entered on a new life. This boy became the very excellent James Kershaw, Esq., M.P.

In both these cases we see much wisdom, great patience, and a pleasing manifestation of Christian piety. If an opposite line of conduct had been adopted what would have been the consequence?

Having fulfilled my month's probation at Lechlade, I received a unanimous invitation to the pastoral office. The people were very urgent, and would not have me say nay. I knew that the good people I had left would feel it exceedingly if I did not return. I knew also that if I consented to stay at Lechlade I should have much more work and much less pay. I was not afraid of work. It was what I had looked after. Everything appeared promising in that respect. The attendance became good, and several persons were brought to Jesus Christ in the early days of Christian effort there, the first fruits of very many more.

I accepted the invitation, and the ordination services were fixed for June 7, 1827. The day came; and with it a large number of Ministers and friends from the churches far and near; Revd D. Wright of Blockley read the lesson and offered up prayer; Revd T. Coles, Bourton on the Water, stated the nature of a gospel church, and asked the usual questions; Revd James Smith, Astwood, offered the ordination prayer, and the Revd R. Pryce of Coate delivered the charge to the young Minister.

Nearly one hundred ministers and friends dined together at the New Inn, where every comfort was carefully provided by the host and his good wife. After dinner several kind and interesting speeches were delivered, abounding with hearty good wishes for the prosperity of the minister, and the people over whom he had taken the oversight. Very affecting references were made to the memory of the late William Fox, Esq., of the Manor House, Lechlade, and the friends of the Baptist interest in the town.

The evening service was good, and an eloquent sermon was preached by the Rev[d] J. Kershaw, Abingdon, being a charge to the church on their duty towards the Minister, and towards each other in the Lord. The whole of the services were interesting, solemn, and profitable.

We insert here the questions proposed and answered, together with the Minister's confession of Faith.

"Do you accept the invitation of this Church to the Pastoral Office?"

"Dear Sir, after much deliberation, and, I trust, fervent prayer to God for direction, I have come to the conclusion to accept the Invitation which has just been read. Difficulties and disappointments I expect to meet with. God, however has promised to all his faithful servants strength according to their day, and, depending upon Divine grace I humbly hope to commend myself to every man's conscience as in the sight of God, to be clear from the blood of all men, and to present many as the fruit of my ministry in the day when Christ shall appear for the redemption of his people.

"The reflection that many around my parish, for lack of knowledge, and impressed as I feel myself with the value of the soul, and the honour and happiness of turning men from darkness unto light, I shall consider no labour, no sacrifice too great, so that I may be instant in season, and out of season; reproving, rebuking, exhorting, with all long-suffering and gentleness. The thought on one hand of any perishing through my un-faithfulness, or inattention to duty, and that after preaching to others I myself may be disapproved, and, on the other hand, the thought that my ministry will prove the savour of death unto death to many of my hearers, fill me with awe, and I do most earnestly entreat your prayers, and those of my Christian brethren present, that I may be found worthy of this all important office."

"Will you give me and this assembly a brief account of the reasons which induced you to enter upon the ministry amongst Protestant Dissenters, and to accept the pastoral charge over this church in particular?"

"From a child I have been the subject of deep convictions, and had my dear parents been, at the time, persons who loved and feared God, I have reason to believe that like a Samuel or a Timothy[3] I should, earlier in life, have devoted myself to God. But, Alas! through their want of spiritual religion, and the depravity of my own heart, the blossom that, in the morning, promised to bear fruit, seemed to wither away.

"Having left the parental roof, at an early age, I found myself, in a certain sense, freed from many restraints, the consequence of which was, that I went to greater lengths in sin than before, which, in itself, I confess, I never fully enjoyed, owing to those early and constant convictions which always had planted thorns in my path of vain pleasures.

"In the year 1819 I made a public profession of the name of Christ. I was received into the Baptist Church at Newtown, Montgomeryshire, under the Pastoral care of the Rev[d] John Jones. In the year 1822 I was called upon by the church to exercise by talents in the ministry, was received upon the Stepney Institution, London, on the 25 of March, 1823, and appointed with others, admitted at the same time, to be placed under the care of the Rev[d] W. Gray of Chipping Norton, Oxon., whose paternal kindness, and valuable instructions I hope I never shall be so ungrateful as to forget.

"I entered, Sir, upon the ministry among Protestant Dissenters because I believe they adhere more closely to the principles of the Bible than the National Established Church of England, and, as a Dissenter from that Church perhaps it may be deemed necessary to state more fully the reasons which have determined my course of conduct.

"Its general frame and constitution is national and established. The character and authority of certain officers appointed in it; the imposition of a stated form of prayers, called the Liturgy, containing much which is, in my opinion, unscriptural; the pretended right of enjoining unneces-

---

[3] The prophet Samuel was the son of Elkanah and Hannah. Hannah was barren and had prayed for a child at the temple of Shiloh, promising to devote him to the service of Yahweh. The young Samuel grew up in Shiloh as a pupil of Eli, the chief priest.

Paul describes Timothy as "a dear son to me and a most trustworthy Christian." [*Corinthians I, 4:17, New English Bible*]

sary ceremonies in religion; the terms on which its ministers are admitted into office; the want of liberty in the people to choose their own minister; and, lastly, the corrupt state of its discipline; all these have presented themselves before my mind as unanswerable objections to communion with that church. However, for many of its ministers and members I entertain the most cordial esteem.

"I cannot but feel grateful for the retreat afforded me by the Societies of the Protestant Dissenters of this country, which though doubtless imperfect in some things, are nevertheless mainly founded upon Holy Writ.

"The circumstances which led me to this part of the Lord's Vineyard have been already detailed in the letter from the church, so as to render a restatement unnecessary.

"Suffer me to say, that I consulted my esteemed tutor, and also many neighbouring ministers and friends, united with fervent prayers to the Great Head of the church for direction, and, seeing that a thorough unanimity seemed to pervade the church and congregation, that an extensive field for usefulness was before me and, the number of our hearers greatly increasing, I was placed in a situation in which I could not answer their unanimous and affectionate invitation in the negative. Consequently, I resolved, in humble dependance on the aid promised to the minister of Christ, to comply with their request, hoping to be faithful unto death, and at last to receive a crown of Life.

"These, my Dear Sir, are some of the dealings of God towards me, in the dispensation of his Providence and Grace."

"Will you give me and this assembly some statements of the sentiments which, in the strength of God you intend inculcating?"

The Confession of Faith. "In complying with your suggestion as I most cheerfully do, nothing more, I apprehend, will be necessary than to draw up a compendious outline of that scheme of sacred truth I firmly believe, and which, in its connexions and influence will furnish the subject of my ministry.

"I am taught by the light of nature the existence of a Supreme Being, that man is dependant upon him for all things and consequently accountable to him for his conduct. Yet though it be true that the invisible things of God, even his eternal power and Godhead, may be clearly seen by the things which are made, the state of the human race is such, and ever has been since the Fall, as to require a more explicit revelation of the Divine will, perfections and purposes. Here Revelation lends its assistance. This is contained in the writings of the Old and New Testaments, which, by way of eminence, is denominated the Bible.

"This holy book, given by inspiration of God, and authenticated by the completest evidence, I receive as the standard of religious sentiment and moral character. Having been, I hope, enlightened by this testimony of the Lord, it will be my humble endeavour to enforce its truths and claims, and from it to derive the instructions I have to communicate.

"From hence I learn, there is but one God, possessed of absolute and infinite perfections who by his Providence governs the world, extending his regards to all his creatures.

"That in the unity of the Divine essence there are three Persons; the Father, the Son, and the Holy Spirit, each of which bear divine names, possess divine attributes, perform divine works, and receive divine honours. As such they must be one in essence, whatever inferiority may exist in point of office in the economy of redemption.

"I believe on the testimony of Holy Writ, that in the beginning God created the Heavens and the Earth, and that the chief object of this sublunary creation was man, who was originally formed in the likeness of his Creator, and rendered amenable to his moral government.

"That man, being left to the freedom of his will, disobeyed the divine precept, and by transgression did involve himself and his posterity in circumstances of guilt, condemnation and ruin.

"I learn that the God of love determined to glorify his perfections in the salvation, and ultimate happiness of a great number of guilty sinners, which no man can number, who were for this glorious end chosen in Christ before the foundation of the world.

"This gracious purpose was gloriously unfolded to man after the fall, till at length, 'in the fulness of time', God sent his own Son into the world, who knew no sin, to become a sin offering for us, to make provision for the honourable bestowment of divine grace, and to offer himself a ransom for the redemption of such as should believe in his name.

"The Eternal Son of God having taken upon him our nature, suffered for us men and for our salvation, magnifying the law, and making it honourable, and opening a medium for the communication of his mercy in agreement with the dictates of infinite wisdom.

"Jesus having died as the surety of his people arose from the dead, thus furnishing an infallible proof that the work which he had declared to be finished was well pleasing to God, and is sufficient in itself to prove him just in justifying the ungodly who believe.

"In consequence of the death and resurrection of Christ, the Holy Spirit is imparted to enlighten men, to create in them new principles, and ultimately to transform them into the divine image, so that by the purpose of God the Father, the mediation of God the Son, and by the energy of God the Holy Spirit, the conversion, progress and final salvation of such who believe are fully secured.

"Nor do I for a moment consider that the secret purpose of God respecting individual salvation can form the rule of human duty.

"I should regard my ministry as essentially defective if I did not urge the unlimited invitations of the Gospel in all their persuasiveness and variety.

"I am, however, deeply convinced that such is the natural aversion of the depraved heart to the Gospel that all persuasion and entreaty will be in vain except accompanied by divine influence. But to all who reject the Gospel, it will be justly laid to their charge. 'Light is come into the world, but men love darkness rather than light, because their deeds are evil.'

"The glorious Gospel when believed is the great means of sanctification, a work which is carried on within the heart, and ends only with the extinction of sin. The progress of this work is rendered in proportion as our understanding is enlightened, our affections become spiritual, and our lives conformed to the will of God and the example of Christ.

"For the accomplishment of the gracious purposes of divine love in the reception of Christ by faith, and to carry on the work of grace in the heart of the believer, God has instituted the Christian ministry as one of the grand and principal means for the conversion, sanctification, and eternal redemption of all the saints.

"The ordinances of the house of God, Baptism and the Lord's Supper, are other means appointed by the King of Zion for the benefit of his subjects.

"Baptism is a standing ordinance in the Church of Christ, and no one is a proper subject for this ordinance who has not a scriptural evidence of being a believer in Christ. The mode of its administration is by immersion. This ordinance I conceive to be a lively representation of the death, burial, and resurrection of Christ, as of the believer's dying with him, and rising to a newness of life.

"The Lord's Supper is an ordinance, in which, by receiving the elements of bread and wine, according to our Lord's appointment, we do shew forth his death, and is doubtless intended to impress our hearts with a lively sense of the evil of sin, and of his own unbounded love.

"Every church and society of Christians is, in its government, wholly independent of every other, and is vested with power to choose its own officers, to receive members, and to expel them, if their conduct be not consistent with the gospel they profess.

"The only officers of the church are pastors and deacons; the one appointed to promote the spiritual welfare of the church, and the other to manage her temporal affairs.

"I believe in the final perseverance of the Saints, for the covenant of grace, the union between Christ and his people, and the precious promise of a faithful God, all united to ensure it. Still, this perseverance, I believe, is always accompanied with the visible effects of divine grace in the life and conduct.

"I believe that the souls of Christians do, immediately on quitting the body, pass into glory, while those of unbelievers are consigned to the abodes of darkness, and reserved to the Judgement of the great day.

"I believe in a future resurrection and judgment, that all the dead shall be raised to appear before the Judge, to receive their final sentence from the lips of Jesus Christ, who will award to the righteous eternal happiness, but to the ungodly everlasting death.

"These, Sir, are the sentiments which, at present, I feel myself required and prepared firmly to maintain. As such, I hold them dear, still leaving my mind open to conviction, and diligently applying to the Holy Scriptures as the source of all truth.

"With a steady adherence to the dictates of conscience, firmly maintaining opinions carefully and scripturally formed, and desirous of cherishing a friendly regard towards all them that love the Lord Jesus Christ in sincerity, I advance to the solemn charge, entreating the prayers of my Christian friends. That God may enable me to perform the duties of the sacred office with a single view to his glory. Thus may one who feels himself to be the unworthiest obtain the approving plaudit of the Divine Master, whose I am, and whom I serve. 'Well done thou good and faithful servant, enter thou into the joy of thy Lord'. Amen. Amen."

I began my work at Lechlade with all the vigour and earnestness of a man who feels that he has a great work to do and did, more or less, continue to follow it up without cessation for above twenty years. It will now be my object to review the labours of the past, in the town and the villages around it. If I have no cause for boasting, I have very abundant cause for gratitude, and thankfulness to God, that he had not withdrawn from me his gracious presence, nor allowed me to labour in vain, and spend my strength for nought.

8

WE HAD A VERY INTERESTING STATION AT FILKINS.

I PREACHED IN this village in a house for some time, where much good was done, but was enabled, soon after, to erect a chapel in the place. Persecution was felt very much for a time, but we moved steadily on, and God did, I believe, overrule all these things for good. I shall give a case or two by way of illustration.

A woman, the wife of a labourer, went to the meeting. When her husband found of it he used her very roughly, and swore that if she went there again he would drag her away by the hair of her head. The woman went again, yes, she dared to do it. When the man found of it he started after her in great wrath. He came to the door, looked in, and saw his wife in the farther part of the room. He appeared as furious as a demon. He advanced to the middle of the room with determined purpose. All at once he stood still, seemed to hesitate and then burst into tears. He sat down and wept till the close of the service. The great work was done. God saved his soul, and made him a monument of mercy, and to us he became one of the most useful men in the church. The good people wanted a person very much to lead the singing. The Lord gave them this man and, in this respect, he was all that could be desired. He had been a singer in the Parish Church for years. He had a good judgment in music, a good voice, and few persons could copy the notes better than he could. He always met me with a cheerful countenance and, when taken ill for death, the good man was resigned, peaceful, and happy. "Mark the perfect man, and behold the upright, for the end of that man is peace."

The press they say, and deny it who can,
That once on a time, in the sacred Divan,
Minerva, the arts and the sciences joined,
She asked them to tell her how man was defined
(N.B. Each gave an opinion.)

Religion spoke last, and all grave was her sentence.
She thought him half angel when brought to repentance.
When faith in Messiah and love spread the leaven
With his nature renewed he was miniature heaven.

Sin made poor William Allen half Devil, Religion made him half angel, and the sovereign purifying influence of Divine grace made him a perfect, glorified spirit. There he stands, pure, bright and happy in the presence of his Divine Redeemer.

Among others received into the church by baptism, soon after my ordination, there was a woman of the name of Mary Cook, a very sincere woman I have no doubt, a widow and a nurse, generally much respected by her neighbours. She had been a church woman, and evidently depended much on human goodness, till she heard me preach a sermon upon the New Birth. She understood it, and felt it. The text was, "except a man be born again, he cannot see the kingdom of God."[1]

Nothing appeared extraordinary to me in her conversion more than in any of those persons admitted into the church at the same time. Nor should I refer to her more than the rest but for the following singular revelation.

Some years afterward she was taken alarmingly ill. No one thought she

---

[1] "Jesus answered, 'In truth, in very truth I tell you, unless a man has been born over again he cannot see the kingdom of God.'

"'But how is it possible', said Nicodemus, 'for a man to be born when he is old? Can he enter his mother's womb a second time and be born?'

"Jesus answered, 'In truth I tell you, no one can enter the kingdom of God without being born from water and spirit. Flesh can give birth only to flesh; it is spirit that gives birth to spirit. You ought not to be astonished then, when I tell you that you must be born over again. The wind blows where it wills; you hear the sound of it, but you do not know where it comes from, or where it is going. So with everyone who is born from spirit.'" [John 3:3-8, New English Bible]

could possibly recover. I went frequently to see her in her illness, and always found her very peaceful and happy in her mind. One day she said,

"Mr. Breeze, as I shall not live long, I have been thinking that I ought to tell you of a peculiar dream I had before you came to reside at Lechlade. It was this. I thought in my dream that some of the good women who go to meeting called upon me and invited me to go with them to hear a young minister who was going to preach. I thought I went, and saw and heard the minister. His text was, 'Except a man &c.' I dreamed that I never felt so impressed in my life. I wept and sobbed aloud and became afterwards so happy, quite a new creature. I awoke and it was a dream, but the picture of the scene I shall never lose sight of.

"I said nothing about it to anyone, but pondered it in my mind, and many times wished it might become true.

"The good women came to invite me to hear a young preacher whom they had heard at Lechlade in the morning. I thought of my dream, and went; but great was my disappointment. The minister was not the man I expected to see, nor was the text the same. Some few months after, I was invited to go again. I went, thinking of my dream. No sooner had I entered the house than I saw the minister, and I should have known him among a thousand. The text was the same, and even some of the hymns sung, the people present, and my conversion. Everything corresponded in a remarkable manner to my dream."

She looked at me, and said, "You were the preacher, Sir. I feel as satisfied as I am of my own existence that the hand of God was in it."

I gave her the best advice I could, and left her, expecting never to see her again in this life. She did get over this illness and lived some years afterward.

This good woman was too true and too honest to practise deception. Besides, she had no inducement to attempt such a thing. That God may, by this method, have prepared her mind to receive the truth, is not at all impossible, nor even improbable. God said by the Prophet Joel, "your sons and your daughters shall prophesy, your young men shall see visions, and your old men shall dream dreams."[2] What we know not now we shall know hereafter.

About twelve months ago I was passing through a street in Faringdon, and a female ran after me, and asked me to go into her house, as she wanted to have a little conversation with me. I had known her from a child; her mother had been a member of our church at Lechlade, and she had been a member of the Baptist church at Faringdon for some years.

"I hope you will excuse my running after you, Sir," she said, "it always does me so much good to see you. I never can forget the sermons you were used to preach at Filkins, and one especially, which I heard when I was quite a little girl."

She told me the text, and, said she, "I remember an anecdote which you related, that caused me many sleepless nights, and many tears, and which was, I believe, the means of my conversion, young as I was then. You said that a very wicked young man dreamed that he had died, and gone to the bad place. There he saw many persons whom he had known in this world, but he saw no fire and brimstone that he had heard so much about when he was on earth. 'You do not seem to suffer much here that I can see,' said he, so one of the young sufferers opened his breast, and shewed a body of fire burning in his bosom, which was terrible to behold. They begged of him to get back to life as soon as possible, and alter his way of living, or he would surely come to that dreadful place and be as miserable as they were. The young man woke up, and found it was a dream, and it appears to have been blessed to him."

"Well," I said, "I can recollect the circumstances, and you must have carried this sermon, and this dream, in your memory for nearly forty years."

"Yes, Sir," said she, "and I never shall forget it. What a mercy I ever heard these things."

I expressed the hope that God would enable her to be faithful unto death, and left, greatly comforted by this unexpected incident, and determined, I trust, to work on and to work always, as long as God employed me in his vineyard. Jesus said, "I must work while it is called today, for the

---

[2] Joel 2:28 [New English Bible]

night cometh when no man can work."

Some four or five years ago, before I came to preach at Filkins, my predecessor Mr. Clarke had a great deal of trouble with some of the lower and baser sort of this village. They did all they could to oppose him, so as to prevent him coming into the place, and sometimes the persecutors were so rough that the lives of the minister and the people assembled were really in danger. These lawless acts were encouraged, it is said, by persons in the locality, who ought to have been the promoters of peace and good order, instead of the disturbers of it. Things came at length to a visit. Mr. Clarke must give up the station, or seek the protection of the law as his life was unquestionably in great jeopardy.

He sought the advice of ministers and friends who said he had better adopt the latter course and they would do all they could to sustain him in whatever action he may take in the matter.

He applied for warrants against some four or five of the ring-leaders of the mob, so they were led up before the magistrates and committed to prison for trial at the next assizes at Oxford. The trial came on, money was collected by the friends of the prisoners to employ counsel. It is said that those persons who had encouraged the rioters most, were the most tardy in their contributions, which disgusted the prisoners and their friends as well as their neighbours in general. But to bring this long and unhappy tale to a speedy termination, I merely state, that two of the fellows were acquitted on their trial and two of them were retained in prison for more than twelve months and then cleared, at the urgent entreaty of Mr. Clarke, the prosecutor.

The mob had been quieted by their failure for some time, but soon after I came, several lewd persons showed unmistakable symptoms of a disposition to renew the struggle, supposing most likely, that I had not spirit enough to resist them. If they did think so, they were evidently mistaken, which they soon found out to their no small mortification.

One night we were in the house engaged in divine service, when a man called out at the door asking if his wife was within, cursing and swearing most awfully, and a number of fellows were outside with him enjoying the fun of it.

I dismissed the congregation, and on inquiry I found that the leader of these wicked men was a veterinary surgeon of the place, a very drunken and abusive fellow. I thought I would wait a little before I took any action in the case, just to see if it was merely a drunken freak, or if he meant something by it. On hearing that, he blustered out all manner of falsehoods against us and many fools believed him. I found it necessary to proceed against the man. He said that we were all a poor lot of Ranters, not worth five pounds altogether, parson and all. That he would give five pounds to anyone for burning down the house in which we met. That we were as ignorant as we were poor and, as a proof of it, he asked the parson where Moses was when the candle went out, but he could not tell, &c. I thought it time for action and had him served with a warrant. The charge was proved against him before the magistrates. These gentlemen urged me to forgive him on condition of his asking my pardon, paying the expenses and promising faithfully never to disturb me again. I pitied him and granted the request. He kept his word and even came to chapel sometimes afterwards and when ill for death he sent for me to read and to pray with him. Since that time not a dog has ever moved his tongue against us.

> I'm not ashamed to own my Lord
> Or to defend his cause;
> Maintain the honour of his word
> The glory of his Cross.
>
> Jesus, my God, I know his name
> His name is all my trust
> Nor will he put my soul to shame
> Nor let my hope be lost.

9

ANCESTRY, MARRIAGE AND FAMILY CONNECTIONS.

I SHALL BEGIN with my venerable Great-Grandfather John Goodwin. I met with a printed Biography of him some years ago in a work called Piety Promoted. I will introduce it just as it is. Every sentence, word, and letter of it is, to me, as precious as gold dust.

John Goodwin, an ancient Friend at *Eskyrgoch* in *Montgomeryshire* in *North-Wales*, was early favour'd with the blessed Visitation of Truth, and by faithfully adhering to the Dictates thereof, he experienced its Effects to be redeeming him, and purifying him as a Vessel for the great Master's Use; so that about the twenty-seventh Year of his Age,[1] he was called to the Work of the Ministry, in which through faithfully and diligently wait-ing for all-sufficient Help, he became an able Minister of the Gospel, and was instrumental to turn many from Darkness to Light, and from the Power of Satan to the Power of God, that he might well be number'd among the Valiants of *Israel*; often visiting the Principality of *Wales*, and in his younger Part of his Live, divers Parts of *England*: He filled up the several Duties of Life with good Repute, being an affectionate Husband, a tender Father, a good Neighbour: Also in a religious Sense, a wise nurs-ing Father, pleasant in Conversation, yet weighty and instructive to those who enquired the Way to Sion; when led to reprove, he was careful to abide in the Spirit of Meekness and Wisdom. He was of an upright Life

---

[1] Transcribed from facsimile of *Piety Promoted*, originally published by John Tomkins in 1701. The life of John Goodwin was contained in the eighth part published in London in 1774. Photocopy provided by the British Museum. If his age when he was called to the ministry, and his age at death is correct, John Goodwin was born *ca* 1681, and would have been twenty-seven *ca* 1708.

and Conversation, a fervent Lover of the Cause of Truth and People of God, zealous of the Honour of Truth and the Support of its Testimony in all its Branches.

In his younger Years, when in low Circumstances, and anxious for the Support of his Family, he purposed removing to *America* (his Parents, Brother and Sisters being gone thither before) but finding a Stop in his Mind, and feeling after Divine Counsel, he found it his Place to settle in his native Land, and it livingly arose in his Heart *that the Lord would provide for him and his Family*, in which he believed; and in the Close of his Days said with Thankfulness, *The Lord had fulfilled it to him*; which is worthy of Commemoration, and may serve as a Way-mark to others who read this Account, to have their Eye to him in Faith, with whom Counsel dwells, for Direction in all their Concerns of Life.

He continued fresh and lively to old Age; and about three Weeks before his Decease, at the last publick Meeting he attended, he was enabled to bear Testimony in the Life and Power of Truth, in a remarkable Manner, to those present, amongst whom were divers not in Society with us; and after the Meeting said, *He was fully clear of the People, and released from that Service;* signifying *his Time here was near a Conclusion, and that, now after a painful Affliction he should soon be at Rest with the Righteous, for which he long'd;* yet said, *Let Patience have its perfect Work.*

During his Illness he appeared to be in an Heavenly Frame of Mind, abounding with Praises to God for his continued Mercies, often excreting how valuable the Enjoyment of the Love of God is on a Dying-bed. He desired his Love might be remembred to his Brethren and Sisters in Christ, being sensible and clear in his Understanding to the last Hour.

He quietly departed this Life, as one falling into a sweet Sleep, the 7th of the Twelfth Month 1763, and was buried in Friends Burial-ground at *Llwyndee*, the 12th of the same. Aged about eighty-two Years.

Let me die the death of the righteous and let my last end be like his.

> Life's labour done, as sinks the day,
> Light from its load the spirit flies;
> While heaven and earth combine to say,
> How blest the righteous when he dies.

It appears that this dear and venerable saint left one only son, Mr. Edward Goodwin, who was married to a Miss Hughes of Llandinan.[2]

She was very respectably connected, and the family of the Hughes through industry and intermarriages with the families of the one respectable class in the neighbourhood, have well maintained that high position to the present day. These family connexions now go under the names of Hughes, Medderis, Wilson, Evans, &c. Most of the chief families in this and the adjoining parishes are related to each other. Some of them are found in the learned professions, in the church, the law and the medical profession. I knew Dr. E___ very well. He was said to be very skilful in his profession. The greatest wag and humourist in the town in which he lived, and as fine an outward man I scarcely ever beheld. He was furnished with the largest nose to his face I ever saw.

One day this gentleman was riding over a bridge. He saw a man with a very large nose coming to meet him on a Welsh pony. He called out hastily to him to keep the other side that the two large nosed might pass each other safely so as to avoid a collision and serious damages. Old Mr. Owen, for that was the man's name, was not up to the joke at the moment, flew into a great passion, and almost shewed fight, till the matter was explained to his satisfaction; when they agreed to have a good, hearty laugh over the large noses.

Mr. M___, an influential Solicitor was also one of the family. He was clever, it was said, in his profession. A great man in his day and one who had great influence in the locality, and was as well trusted in the weighty matters of the law as most gentlemen. I do not say dishonesty is essential to that respectable profession. Why should it be so? An honest man is a man of sterling worth wherever he is found.

Now these incidents with many others are associated with my boyhood, I feel induced to name them as I pass along, altho' few persons may think as much of them as myself.

My grandfather and grandmother occupied a farm near the village of

---

[2] Edward Goodwin of Trefeglwys, singleman and Susan Hughes of this parish were married by banns 13 October 1755 *[Llandinam Bishop's Transcripts]*

Llandinam, but it does not appear that my grandfather walked in the steps of his worthy and devout father John Goodwin of happy memory. Through marrying out of the Society he became separated from them, according to their over-rigid rules and, there being no Quakers in the place, it is most probable that he became indifferent to godliness and lived like the rest of his neighbours, "without God and without hope in the world."

However God woke him from this state of spiritual slumber by a very remarkable dream. He dreamed that he was at a gay party, all being very cheerfully engaged, when he heard a carriage drive up to the door, and that Mr. Edward Goodwin was wanted. He thought that he tried to excuse himself, but he must go to the door, there was no excusing himself. The fact was this, that he had suddenly the impression made on his mind, even in his dream, that this was a message to him from the invisible world and that he felt unprepared to receive it. He went at length, he thought, with much fear to the door, when a grave-looking gentleman put his head through the window of the coach and said,

"I am come to fetch you and I hope you are ready to go with me."

He felt much alarmed and said, "no, Sir, I am not ready."

"Then," said the stranger, "see to it. This night twelvemonths, and at this hour, I will come again," and then drove off.

This singular dream had such effect upon him that it awoke him and the clock then struck the hour of one in the morning.

He considered this a direct warning from heaven and a presentiment of his approaching end. He laid this matter so much to heart that he spent a great part of the year in earnest prayer to God and in great soul-searching, in hopes indeed that he might be ready to meet his Lord at his coming. It was in vain for his friends to tell him that it was only a dream, for his mind was intently fixed upon his purpose, and no one could drive him away from it.

Just before the end of the year, the little children, four in number, my mother being one of them, were taken ill of the smallpox and, as the young father had never had that sad malady, he also was taken alarmingly ill, and became worse and worse just as the fatal hour approached.

As the time came near, he expressed a wish to kiss the children. They were brought and, having taken his leave of all, he solemnly and cheerfully clasped both his hands together and committed his soul into the hands of God, and breathed his last in this life.[3] This is the account I received from my dear mother, when I was young, and having had it oft repeated, I feel pretty confident of the above statements being correct. I cannot account for it. Was it the power of imagination? Or was it in answer to his good father's prayers? I should think it was the latter. God is not confined to one method in answering the sincere prayers of his people. "What we know not now, we shall know hereafter."

My own dear father was born in the parish of Llanbrynmair, Montgomeryshire, at a farm house called *Coidlynain*. There were three children, and the parents dying when they were young, they had to begin early the battles of life as best they could. God who becomes the Father of the fatherless stood their friend, so that through mercy they did very well.

I went once to visit my relatives in that neighbourhood and found those upon whom I called in well-to-do circumstances and very religious. Finding that I was, at the time, under deep convictions of sin, they spoke to me very kindly and urged me much to give my heart and service to God without delay. These visits did me good.

Several of my father's kindred rose to some eminence in the world and in the Church, so that I have often to feel thankful for the time-honoured name of Breeze. I hope I never shall live to dishonour it. E. Breeze, Esq., London, Barrister at Law and of the firm of Coventry, Breeze & Co. was one of the kindred. The Rev[d] John Breeze[4] of Liverpool, who, together

---

[3] Edward Godwin of Lower Mill, buried 7 June 1763, at Llandinam. Three children of Edward and Susannah Godwin were baptized at Llandinam: Susannah, daughter of Edward Goodwyn, of Triwythen, weaver and Susan his wife, baptized 17 March 1758; Jane, the daughter of Edward Goodwyn, millar, by Susannah his wife, baptized 12 October 1760 or 1761; Ursula the daughter of Edward Godwin and Susanna his wife, Lower Mill, baptized 21 July 1763. *[Llandinam Bishop's Transcripts]*

[4] I have not discovered a relationship between the Rev. John Breeze and Richard Breeze. Brees, Breese or Breeze is a very common name in that area of Montgomeryshire. "Breese, John, 1789-1842, a Congregational preacher, was born at Llanbrynmair, Montgomeryshire. He received but little education in early life, and for some time he was employed as a farm labourer. When 24 years of age, having, in the meantime, commenced to preach, he was sent to Shrewsbury School, and afterwards to college. He then settled down as pastor in Liverpool, where he laboured with great success for 17 years. He spent

with my old friend Williams of Wern, were for a time two of the most eminent ministers in the Congregational denomination. Mr. John Breeze afterwards became copastor with the renowned Mr. Peters of Caermarthon, and finally his successor in the pastorate of the largest Independent Church in Wales. I once had the pleasure of preaching in the pulpit he, for years, ably occupied. I saw also the tomb that covered the ashes of the dear departed brother–I name at present the last but not the least of these worthies–the Rev[d] Samuel Breeze[5] of Aberystwith, who, with the Rev[d] Christmas Evans[6],

---

the last seven years of his life at Carmarthen. He travelled much, and among the people of his own denomination was considered second only to Williams of Wern as a preacher. He was exceptionally liberal in his views as a Nonconformist, so much so that during his pastorate in Liverpool, Dr. Bethell, then Bishop of Bangor, wrote offering to ordain him as minister of the Church of England, and subsequently sent a neighbouring clergyman to Liverpool specially to endeavour to persuade him to take orders in the Church, but he declined. His sermons were mainly doctrinal, and, at times, only the most intelligent of his hearers could follow him with any profit." *[Eminent Welshmen : a short biographical dictionary of Welshmen who have attained distinction from the earliest times to the present /* Roberts, T. R., 1908]

[5] Samuel Brees, bap. 5 October 1772, son of John Brees of Carnidd and Elizabeth Stevens *[Llandinam Bishop's Transcripts]* May not be correct Samuel.

"Breese, Samuel, 1772-1812, a Baptist minister, was born at Llandinam, Montgomeryshire. In his eighth year, he became lame, and this induced his parents to give him a better education than they would otherwise have done. For some time he followed the occupation of schoolmaster, but in 1795 he began to preach. He became one of the most popular and powerful preachers of the day, and in 1803 became co-pastor at Aberystwyth with the Rev. John James. He afterwards removed to Newcastle Emlyn, where he laboured with much success. His descriptive powers were remarkably vivid, and few preachers were more eloquent and popular. He travelled much throughout Wales and parts of England, preaching fluently in English as well as Welsh. He was buried in the burial ground attached to the old Baptist Chapel at Cilfowyr, Pembrokeshire. Elegies were written on his death by the Revs. D. Saunders and Christmas Evans, and the latter was reprinted in the form of a pamphlet at Llanidloes in 1846." *[Eminent Welshmen, op. cit.]*

[6] "Evans, Christmas, 1766-1838, a Baptist minister, was born at Ysgarwen, in the parish of Llandyssil, Cardiganshire, on Christmas day, 1766. His parents were not in a position to pay for his education, and, when about seventeen years of age, he became farm servant to the Rev. David Davies, Castle Howel, where he was initiated into the rudiments of learning. He was induced to commence preaching, and joined the Arminian Presbyterians, but preached also occasionally with the Independents and Baptists. He afterwards threw in his lot with the Baptists, and became one of the most powerful preachers of the day. In 1791 he settled at Llangefni, Anglesey, removing in 1826 to Caerphilly, in Glamorganshire, and 1832 to Carnarvon, where he remained till his death. His striking imaginative style, and lively theatrical action in preaching, rendered him exceedingly popular. He travelled much throughout the Principality, stirring the hearts of the people, and producing mighty results. For vigorous thought, rich imagination, and picturesque

were the wonder of the age in which they lived. These were two of the brightest stars in the Baptist Denominations.

As I had been early in life made acquainted with the good people called Quakers, or Friends, I was led to admire them exceedingly. Their quiet and gentle manners and the neatness of their attire and the loveliness of their disposition, together with the undeniable excellence of my never-to-be-forgotten maternal grandparents, brought an occasional stray wish into my mind to know more of these good people. The ladies of this section of the Christian Church, I admired very much. I justly inferred when the outward appearance was so modest and retiring, their dress so neat and so void of outward show, that their minds must be richly endowed with useful knowledge and the fear of the Lord. Under these impressions I could not feel reconciled to anything showy, gaudy and flashy as is sometimes seen. Ladies arrayed in all the trickery of dress and covered with jewels, dangling pendants &c. as if on purpose to excite the gaze and admiration of beholders must, in my opinion, have little minds, and less religion.

I went with my late worthy brother, the Revd D. Wright of Blockley, to the ordination of brother Miles, at Stow on the Wold. We went over the day before, intending to hear a good brother who was expected to preach there on the previous evening. He was not able to come, and I, being a stranger, was requested to take the service. The ordination services the next day were remarkably good and profitable. In the afternoon whilst Mr. Wright and I were walking in the street we met three young ladies, to whom he introduced me, merely as a matter of courtesy. They were tall, handsome and good looking and remarkably neat in their attire. Their appearance altogether indicated minds well-informed and endowed with right principles, just the type of ladies to satisfy my scruples and to meet my preconceived notions of female excellence. I afterwards asked my friend who those young ladies were.

---

language, he had few equals. He was the author of several religious and controversial tracts in Welsh, and a few excellent hymns. He was also one of the translators of Dr. Gill's Exposition of the New Testament into Welsh. A volume of his "Allegories", with a sketch of his life, appeared in 1864 (Liverpool : Isaac Foulkes), and his works, in three volumes, edited by the Rev. Owen Davies, D.D., were published in 1895-7 (Carnarvon : W. Gwenlyn Evans)" [*Eminent Welshmen , op. cit.*]

"They are," said he, "the Misses Beckingsale, of Longborough. We are invited to their house to tea tomorrow. It is in that village that you have to preach tomorrow evening."

This information was given in an offhand way, as if there was nothing important in it, but it was not received with a feeling of indifference by me. My private impression was this; that I had there and then seen my wife in the person of one of those young ladies. We went over on the morrow and, having seen more of the young people, I left under the impression that I should meet them again. Not a word was said, nor even a whisper uttered yet, singular to say, as I found out years afterwards, the impression made on our two hearts was mutual. Who will say after this that matches are not made in heaven? Especially when I say that we did not see each other again for two long years and, down to that time, not a word was said by either party upon the subject, nor by any one else, yet the unuttered wish was still hidden in each heart. When I felt at liberty to make an offer of marriage, I obtained an interview with the lady and in due time I received a favourable reply; but, owing to certain obstacles in the way, we had to wait five years longer.

It is said that you cannot wait too long for a good wife, and that you cannot wait too long for a bad one. However, I found myself, in this matter, on the right side, through mercy. The wedding day was at length fixed, being seven years from the day we first saw each other, and five years from the day of our engagement.[7]

I went down the previous day to Cheltenham, where the beloved one had stayed for some little time with a kind brother. That evening he went with me to the house of the Vicar, the Rev[d] F. Close (now Dean of Carlisle) to get the marriage license and, while preparing it, he asked me how I spelt my name. I told him.

"Oh," said he, "if you have a large family you will be able to raise a storm. I have been married ten years and have now eight children."

"Well, Sir," I said, "if you get on a few years more with equal success,

---

7 Richard Breeze married Sarah Beckingsale, 3 August 1830 in St. Mary, Cheltenham, by license.

you will have a good-sized farm bye and bye." (A *close* is a little field.) At this he laughed outright and so did my brother-in-law, pleased with the sudden retort.

The next morning witnessed the celebration of the happy union which we had so long anticipated and, in the afternoon we directed our course to Lechlade, which was destined for a time to be the place of our dwelling and the scene of much labour and of considerable success. We were cautious and careful and did not make a long and expensive tour merely to exhibit the bridal dress and the white gloves &c for the amusement of lookers on, in obedience to an unwise custom, which prevails so generally at the present day. We arrived safely in the evening at our new home and were soon greeted with the musical bells and a friend or two, who just called in to give us their early benediction.

My dear wife was the youngest daughter of the late Mr. William Beckingsale of Longborough, Gloucestershire, a worthy gentleman, who brought up a large family, very respectably, without the aid of business or profession and, did, by his good management and by the assistance of one of the best and most religious of wives, increase his property rather than diminish it. He was enabled to help his children to enter upon the business of life whenever that help was wanted. This he always did as a matter of business and parental pleasure and he had the happiness of seeing his beloved children thankful, industrious and successful. He was a good man, a member of the Church of England and attended the ministry of the Rev^d Mr. Jones of Evenlade, a distance of three miles, and he scarcely ever failed in his attendance.

Mrs. Beckingsale was a member of the Baptist Church at Stow, a truly pious woman, who was always seen, Sabbath after Sabbath, directing the steps of her beloved children to the little Baptist Chapel at Stow. The good man considered infant baptism to be a useless and unmeaning ceremony, a mere relic of the dark ages, and that religion was a personal thing; so he left his children to act out their convictions when they arrived at years of maturity and discretion. No doubt these judicious views of the father suited the Baptist mother to admiration and did the children no harm, as they nearly all sympathized with their beloved mother in her views of Divine truth early in life, and adopted them. It is very manifest that God gave the gentleman a good share of common sense and he did himself great credit by making a good use of the blessing.

The children of these worthy parents have always been very united and affectionate to each other and, I can testify that, ever since I have had the happiness to be one of the family, they have all treated me with the greatest respect and brotherly kindness. I am exceedingly pleased to be able to state that the grand-children follow closely in the footsteps of their worthy and beloved grandparents in carefulness, industry &c. and, above all, that most of them are directing their course towards the better Land into which so many of their family have safely entered and who are now enjoying the sweet luxury of the glorious Rest. May we all meet there at last! as there is no reason whatever why there should be one of us missing when the Lord shall come to make up his jewels.

A Wedding Hymn. Berridge
Thou who at Cana didst appear
To bless a marriage feast,
Vouchsafe thy gracious presence here,
Be thou with us a guest.

Upon the bridal pair look down,
Who now have joined hands.
Their union with thy favour crown
And bless the nuptial bands.

With gifts of grace their hearts endow
Of all rich dowries best.
Their substance bless and peace bestow
To sweeten all the rest.

In purest love their souls unite
That they with Christian care
May make domestic burdens light
By taking mutual share.

10

THE NEW CHAPEL ERECTED AT FILKINS, OXON, 1832

HAVING ENTERED MORE fully into the engagements of our social and spiritual life, I and my young wife felt very wishful to do all the good we could in the sphere in which God had placed us. Our attention was especially directed to the village of Filkins. Good had been done and we found it imperative to get a chapel to accommodate the people who wished to hear the Gospel. We heard, after much enquiry, that a person had property in a convenient situation, and that he would not object to sell it. Having secured the property, we set to work to improve it by fitting up four houses upon it, in addition to the one already there, making altogether five houses, reserving a suitable piece of land in the further end of the garden for the chapel. I then submitted the matter to my friends in the neighbourhood and to the ministers and the churches in the Oxfordshire Association. All of them urged me to advance with the good work and said that they would do the best they could to assist me in the undertaking; in this they did a good and honourable part, although no one would take a personal responsibility in the matter with me. I was therefore the only responsible man in the business and I went about the work with all my might, my good wife doing all she could to hold up my hands, when, through weariness, they seemed inclined to hang down. At length the building was completed and ready for opening, and it certainly was a model village chapel and much admired by all who saw it. It stood up well, with front gallery, baptistry, vestry; with an iron fence in front of the building and all conveyed into the hands of trustees for the use of the Baptist Denomination for ever. The whole of the expense, amounting to about £300, I collected, with some difficulty, as a matter of course, but it was done, for the good hand of the Lord was upon me. Thanks be to my great Friend, I have had the pleasure of baptizing nearly 100 persons in that place of worship, most, or all of them, the fruit of my ministry in this village and the neighbour-hood. How true the words of Eternal truth, "he that goeth forth weeping, bearing precious seed shall doubtless come again rejoicing, bringing his sheaves with him."

The day of opening was a cheerful and high day with us. Christian friends came from various quarters to cheer us with their smiles and give us their benediction. The ministers present and those who took part in the opening services were: the Revd T. Coles, Bourton on the Water; T. Catton, Chipping Norton; R. Pryce, Coate; E. Lewis, London; B. Hall, Burford; D. Williams, Fairford, &c. The weather was all that could be desired till nearly the close of the evening service, when we had one of the most fearful storms I ever witnessed. The thunder was terrible, the lightning was awful, the rain came down as if poured out of buckets and continued so for hours. We could not leave for our homes till about 3 or 4 o'clock in the morning. A night to be much remembered!

Some time after this the Duchess of Beaufort and Colonel Kingscote sent their tract-missionary to Lechlade, to supply us with tracts and to do all the good he could among us. He wished to see my village stations so we rode off together and in passing by this new chapel he stopped to admire. He asked me if this cluster of villages had good day and Sunday schools in them and I said, "No, not one worth naming."

"Well," said he, "if you will allow the use of the chapel for that purpose I will try to get the Duchess to defray most of the expense and I know a good man who would conduct it."

I could not refuse so good an offer. It was soon arranged and the teacher came, Mr. Andrew Walsh. For some time the school went on well but, alas! The clergy in the neighbouring parishes wrote to the lady about the school and the supplies were soon withheld. We tried it on a little lon-ger but with much difficulty. At length the Colonel engaged Mr. Walsh for a tract missionary and we parted with him very reluctantly and regretfully.

If the school failed the Gospel did not; much good was done and continued to be done for many years.

11

THE VILLAGE OF LANGFORD, BERKSHIRE

I PREACHED SUCCESSFULLY in this village for some years, in conjunction with my other stations. In 1827 I went there first to preach in a house, but many of the people in the place were half mad in their opposition and were encouraged, it is said, by some of the more influential people of the neighbourhood. Stones and all manner of missiles have been thrown against the door, the windows have been broken time after time, so that it really cost us a good deal for damages done. We felt determined to wear them out. The good people felt alarmed, it is true, about my safety and some of them went with me part of the way back each time, but, singular to say, I had no fears at all. I felt physically strong and I believe if it came to life for life, I should have made a terrible resistance but, through mercy, it never came to that. I felt morally strong as I knew that I was engaged in a good work and I had the promise of the divine protection. What had I therefore to fear? If God be for us who can be against us? Promises like these are unfailing comforts to the mind when assailed by rough and noisy insults like these coming as they did, in the dark night, from low blackguards, who did not fear God nor regard man.

I had soon to see fruit from my labour. The good man and his wife in whose house we met, with some others were baptized and good impressions were made on the minds of many persons, and the uproar in the village became a little hushed down and less noisy.

The good man, James Rodway, in whose house I preached, told me one day about some of his difficulties and sought my advice. He had been accustomed to receive his week's wages on Sunday mornings and he very properly thought this wrong. I told him to do the best he could in his work, to be very gentle and obliging in his behaviour and when he saw the master in a good humour, to ask him as a great favour to pay him his wages on Friday or Saturday instead of Sunday morning. One day he ventured to try the great man upon the subject, but, no, I will not repeat what was said nor pollute my pages with the rude and unfeeling words used. It grieved me much to see this awful desecration of the Sabbath and I felt determined to put a stop to it, if I possibly could. I called one day upon the Vicar of Lechlade, a kind man and a perfect gentleman. I named the object of my call, how badly the holy day was violated, that it was an awful fact that in the sight of his own door the shops were open on Sabbath mornings, that groups of customers came from the villages to make their purchase and then went to the public houses and that the shopkeepers would rush off to church and sometimes not get in till the service was half-over.

"Well, Sir, it is true," said he, "and a painful state of things it is, but I cannot help it."

"Dear Sir," said I, "allow me to say that I cannot help it on account of your greater influence but that you can do it with the greatest ease. For instance, if you call upon Mr. G___, the largest farmer in the parish, and tell him of this great evil and request him, as a special favour, to pay his labourers of Friday evenings instead of Sunday mornings, he will do it and be pleased with an opportunity to oblige you, and all the rest you can easily get to do the same. Sir, you can do this blessed work and if you will not use that moral power which God has given you, he will hold you responsible, as the clergyman of this parish, for all the great evil committed here from Sabbath to Sabbath."

"Sir, I am much obliged to you," said he, "and will enquire into it without delay."

The good work was soon done; then I went out to the farmers in the villages and succeeded with them, and really a new state of things took place all around us. Many thanks to him who gave us this blessed day and for putting good thoughts into my mind and prudence to carry them out so successfully!

If I had gone about this work sooner I might have retained a useful family or two who were too conscientious to open their shops on the Sabbath day and who had left the town recently, thoroughly disgusted with this sad state of things. It is true that I had not been in the place long, and it is possible, no doubt, to be over hasty, as the proverb says, "The more haste, the less speed."

There was one marked providential circumstance which I ought not to pass over. A youth, the son of the largest and perhaps the wealthiest farmer in the village happened to come with the shepherd man one evening to hear me preach, and he said afterwards that he was never so much surprised in his life.

"Why," said he, "Mr. Breeze prayed and preached without a book. I never heard anything equal to it in the church." He wished his parents to come and hear me, and said also that he would not go to church any more. As a matter of course the parents felt very vexed about it at the time, but what was to be done? Here is an only son, a little indulged and self-willed, it may be, the only son of the clergyman's churchwarden, who would not go to church, nor could he be compelled to go there! What next? I was agreeably surprised one week evening at seeing the parents walk into the humble edifice to unite with us in the sacred service. At the close, I spoke freely to them and said I was glad to see them and hoped they would come again. I should almost as soon have expected to see the tower and porch of the old church walk up side by side to the Nonconformist Conventicle as to see this gentleman and his good wife come there.

The next time I went, there they were again, and did not I silently and earnestly lift up my heart in prayer to God for them? While I was preaching, I saw the tears roll down the fine, manly face of James Tombs, Esq., for that was the gentleman's name. From that hour he and his excellent lady stood by us and did much to help us to improve the state of things in the parish and locality in general, and did not cease in their noble endeavours to do good, till the day of their departure from earth to heaven. "Be there faithful unto death and I will give thee a crown of life."

Some little time after that he said to me that he felt very anxious for the salvation of his relatives and the more respectable parties in the place, as well as for the humbler portion thereof, as the former would not like to attend service at the cottage in which we met.

"Now," said he, "if you will give us one sermon on the Sabbath day as well as the one service on the week evening, I will fit up a barn, very conveniently situated, for a chapel. I will do it all at my own expense and fit it up neatly and comfortably so that no one need feel ashamed to come into it."

His countenance brightened, and that of his wife too, at the anticipated pleasure of doing the desired good and I felt considerable regret that I could not possibly, at the time, comply with their wishes. Some time after, my good friend Mr. Walsh came again into the neighbourhood, to help me in these village stations.

"Mr. Tombs," I said to him one day, "you have heard my friend Mr. Walsh preach, how do you like him?"

"Yes," said he, "I have heard him and have been agreeably surprised. I like him very well and can hear him with profit and pleasure at any time."

"Do you, Sir, remember a challenge you gave me once?"

"Yes," said he, "I do."

"Well," replied I, "if you are still of the same mind, I will promise you one sermon, if not two every Sabbath, either by myself, or Mr. Walsh."

"Agreed," said he, "and I will go about the work next week."

He did go about it and made a capital job of it too. The new chapel was opened and well filled with hearers, and a great and glorious work was done there that filled many a heart with gladness.

Since that period the good people have built a respectable chapel, they have a day and Sunday School, a good church, and have had now for nearly twenty years, a stated pastor, living in a pastor's house fitted up expressly for him. They have also in their kindness assisted the Primitive Methodists to build a chapel near them, with which body they carry on a holy rivalry in doing good. I hear also that the worthy vicar of the parish is one of the best and most liberal-minded of men, and that the three congregations live in love with each other, and carry on, in beautiful harmony, the great warfare with sin and the wicked one, in which they are severally engaged.

We talk much about the millennium. Why, if we compare Langford now, with what it was when I first knew it, I should say that the glorious era has more than dawned already. I had the honour of ploughing up the hard soil and sowing the seed, and the present reapers have the happiness of gathering in the abundant harvest.

> Stand up, stand up for Jesus! The strife will not be long;
> This day the noise of battle, the next the victor's song:
> To him that overcometh, the crown of life shall be,
> He with the King of Glory, shall live eternally.

12

LITTLE FARINGDON, BERKSHIRE

MR. RICHARD BANTING, a good, simple-hearted man, and better off than some of his neighbours, allowed me to preach in his house, but here we were so roughly assailed, that I feared we should have been obliged to discontinue the services. The poor old man complained about his broken windows and other unpleasant annoyances and felt disposed to give up. I said to him that I would see all the damages repaired and, if we continued the services, most likely the disturbers of our peace would get weary ere long, or that we might be able to make an example of a few of them; that things could not continue long in this state; still, that if he wished me not to come again, I would not. The poor old man burst into tears and said,

"Oh, Sir! Go on. I will not shut my door against Jesus Christ." We did go on and Jesus Christ often came and blessed us and gave us peace. There can be no doubt of this.

Some years ago a sister of Mr. Banting went to London to live and was fortunate in getting a good situation. She was said to be a good-looking, bright, healthy, country girl. A nobleman, Lord C__, actually fell in love with her and felt determined, if possible, to make her his wife. His lordship called upon her employers one day, to make enquiries about her character, morals, disposition, &c. He received very satisfactory replies to his questions, then he told them that his intentions were perfectly honourable. After an interview or two with the young girl they were married and, from all that I have ever heard, they have lived very comfortably together.

I was rather amused with one of neighbour Banting's adventures. One day it came into his head to pay a visit to his young nephews who were at

College at Oxford. He prepared for the journey, being well equipped with cord breeches, worsted stockings, large, heavy shoes well greased, a coat the worse for wear, a large slouching hat, and a strong rough walking stick in his hand. He enters the classic city somewhat weary, after a twenty-five mile walk. He goes direct to the College in which the young gentlemen pursued their studies. He enters the quadrangle, goes to the nearest door and beats it lustily with his great staff. A servant man appears.

"What do you want, old fellow?" said he.

"Want," said he, "I want to see my nephews to be sure, Lord C__ and his younger brother. Tell them that their uncle Richard Banting, Little Faringdon, is come all the way to see them."

The servant went to the rooms occupied by the young gentlemen and said to the elder, "My lord, there is a crazy old man in the quadrangle who says that he is your uncle and has come from Little Faringdon on purpose to see you."

"Very well," said the gentleman, "I will see him."

He went down and spoke kindly to the old man and walked him out into the street, put three or four sovereigns into his hand and said, "Go and get some refreshment, and then go home as soon as you can, as we cannot invite you into our rooms, and I must request you never to come to see us again."

The good man returned home weary with his long journey, but pleased enough with the shining metal in his purse. His sister, her ladyship, sent him a letter containing some wholesome advice afterwards, so he became careful not to offend his greatest earthly friend again.

I wrote to her ladyship once or twice, after the death of poor Banting, on behalf of his widow.

This village, being but one mile from Lechlade, several of the people attended our chapel there.

I had the offer of a house called Little Faringdon Cottage, a good house, garden, stabling and full three acres of good meadow-land, very conveniently situated and at a moderate rent. We came there to live. It was situated at an easy distance from my village stations and from the Lechlade Chapel. I kept here a pony and two cows and found it very agreeable and profitable.

My walks to the different stations had been laborious and solitary, espe-cially in returning home after the late services; I had doubtless some narrow escapes. One time in returning along a solitary part of the road, a rough looking fellow came from under a high hedge right across the road to meet me and stood in the centre of it. I grasped my sturdy stick and walked off briskly, bearing to the left hand side of the road. No one spoke as I remem-ber but, on glancing back, I saw the fellow still in the same place. It looked as if he meant mischief, but I cannot say. At another time a man overtook me just on this spot and asked me how far it was to Lechlade

"Nearly three miles," said I.

"What a devil of a long mile the last was," said he. I repeated his words slowly and solemnly, saying that I never heard of such a mile before.

"Sir," said he, "I ask your pardon. I ought not to have spoken as I did. I know better and sincerely thank you for your kind reproof." He wept very much and said that he had been a hardened backslider for some years. He had been, he said, a member of the Wesleyan Church and even a class leader for a long time, but he had forsaken God, "and God," said he, "has forsaken me, Sir; the words you spoke cut me to the heart and I believe God put those words into your mouth in mercy to my poor soul." He wept excessively and asked me if there was any hope. I gave him the best advice I could and urged him to seek God's forgiving mercy through Jesus Christ, and to go to the good people whom he had so much grieved and seek their prayers and forgiveness too. I asked him also if he had money to pay for his lodging.

"Sir," said he, "I can do for tonight but, if I had none I would sooner lie under a hedge all night than take anything of you, lest you might doubt the sincerity of my contrition and my heart." He parted with me very re-luctantly indeed.

I was one evening returning from our chapel at Filkins on my pony when, in Broughton Lane, I passed four fellows, two, from what I can recollect, standing by the hedge and the other two walking before abreast. Just at that moment some carpenters, &c. came in sight round a bend in the road and this, no doubt, saved me from those horrible fellows who proved themselves that night to be highway robbers. I was informed the next morning that these fellows robbed Messrs Myers of Langford and Little Faringdon within sight of the pike as you enter Lechlade. This took place about an hour after I passed them on the road. These two gentlemen were returning from Fairford Fair and saw four men on the road side, two appeared to be fighting and the other two acting as seconds. The driver unwisely pulled up, when they darted upon them in an instant. One took hold of the horse, two jumped one on each step of the gig and the other grasped the son from behind and nearly broke his back across the bow of the gig. The fellows did their work in about two minutes and started the horse off [at] full gallop. Three or four men standing at the pike came up, hearing a noise, but knowing not what it meant, stood close by the fellows and might have taken them with ease if they had known that they were robbers: then the fellows fired off a pistol, jumped through the smoke right over the hedge into the fields and escaped. The booty amounted to some £10 in cash and the two watches the gentlemen had in their pockets. One of these rascals was taken for this offence and was transported, and two more were soon afterwards transported for a subsequent offence. "The way of transgressors is hard."

I was lately at the Swindon Station and saw twelve or fourteen convicts in chains standing up in a row under the charge of their keepers, waiting for their train, and a lady said,

"Oh, dear!, how sorry I am to see them."

"Very likely, madam," I replied, "but I would sooner see them here than meet them alone in a solitary lane on a dark night. Wholesome laws are good. What should we do without them?"

One night soon after we went to reside at Little Faringdon Cottage, we heard a loud voice in the night in front of the house.

"Bless you," cried some one, "come down immediately to help me. There are two men drowning in the water. God bless you, come down and help them out."

"Who are they? And who are you?" said I, "Satisfy me on that point and I will venture my life to help you." He then swore like a man drunken or in a terrible fright. I did know what he said.

"If you will not tell me," I said, "I will not go with you. You can, if you like, go to the mill there and get the millers to go." I began to question the truth of his statement and thought that he might be a robber or some bad fellow. We were getting up to prepare for whatever might come next, when I saw someone passing by with him, as we could, in the dark, see the shadow of two persons go by. This was a relief in case the statement were true. In two or three minutes afterwards, I heard a loud shout at the water and got the lantern lighted to go and see what it could really mean, when I saw a man come near with three horses, calling out most frantically for help.

"Who are you?" I asked. "My name is F_," he replied. I was down at the door in an instant.

"Put these three horses in the stable and follow me to the bridge," he said, "I fear the men are drowning. Give me the light," and off he went. I put two of the horses in the stable, the third, a spirited fellow, would not go in, so I jumped on his back and was soon down at the water and saw the gentleman dancing on the margin of the water, evidently afraid to go in. (The fact, evidently, was that they were all drunk together.) I could also see two heads above the water. When he saw me on the horse he took hold of the reins and I walked into the water and soon brought the two gentlemen to land. One was an old man above 70 years of age, the other a young man. The next thing to do was to get them up to my house. Mr. F__ and I took the old gentleman by each arm, the horse was led, and the young man took hold of his tail. In this fashion we got up to Little Faringdon Cottage. It would have been a comical sight had there been any one to see it. We had much to do to get heat and vigour into the old man's limbs, however, they were able to go home on the following afternoon, and full of thankfulness they were. The old man said over and over again that, if there was a good Samaritan in the world, I was the man. When the old squire went next to London, he bought a silver cup, to present to my first born son with his initials engraved upon it.[1]

---

[1] William Beckinsale Breeze was born at Little Faringdon on the 8th December 1831 [Information from letter of A.J. Baxter, Lechlade to L. Breeze, 19th December 1975]. The silver cup is still in the family.

Christening cup given to Richard Breeze

The numerous tales circulated through the neighbourhood concerning this disaster were truly amusing. Here is one.

Mr. G____said, "no one would venture into the water to get them out, till Mr. Breeze, the parson, came. He came to the side of the water, said a short prayer, and bravely dashed in and soon brought them out. He is a brave and courageous man."

One Sabbath, a bad man of Lechlade, spread the report in the town, that I was dead and that he had seen me fall off my horse, and that the body was carried to Little Faringdon. The people thought this possible, as I stood engaged to preach at Filkins in the morning and at Lechlade in the afternoon and evening. The excitement was immense. The whole town was moved. Parties called to enquire. At length one of the deacons called and said that the people were so excited and would not believe anything till they saw me, and he urged me to go as soon as possible. I went, and what a sight presented itself! The road was full of men, women and children, and as I entered the town, both sides of the street were lined with people; some wept, others smiled, and all looked surprised and pleased as if, they saw for once at least, a man risen again from the dead. The chapel was crowded and I took advantage of the circumstance and preached a solemn and earnest sermon upon the importance of preparedness to die. A deep and general impression was produced, and I have no doubt that the devil found himself outwitted in this matter. God often brings good out of seeming evil. He is his own interpreter and he will make it plain. Balaam[2] tried to curse the people of Israel, but God compelled him to bless them instead. Blessed is he that has the God of Jacob for a refuge.

Ebenezer[3] by Fawcett

I my Ebenezer raise
To my kind Redeemer's praise.
With a grateful heart I own
Hitherto Thy help I've known.

What may be my future lot,
Well I know concerns me not.
This shall set my heart at rest,
What Thy will ordains is best.

I my all to Thee resign.
Father! let Thy will be mine.
May but all Thy dealings prove
Fruits of Thy paternal love. Amen.

---

[2] Numbers 22-25

[3] 'Ebenezer' means "stone of help" in Hebrew. The Philistines had defeated the Israelites and captured the Ark. They kept it for twenty years. Finally, the Israelites defeated the Philistines. "There Samuel took a stone, and set it between Mizpah and Jeshanah, naming it Ebenezer, 'for to this point', he said, 'the Lord has helped us.'" [I Samuel, 7:12, *New English Bible*]

13

Downington House, Lechlade.
Scholastic Duties

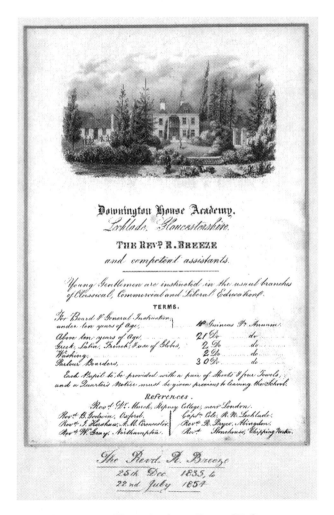

Downington House Academy, Fees and References

This is indeed a world of changes and we have not been free from them at Lechlade. We have, in the order of Divine Providence, in a short space of time, lost four or five of our best supporting and most useful families from our chapel. My own family, also was increasing apace and bye and bye the children would need an education, &c. I might get a situation more calculated to meet the increased demands of my family, I had no doubt, but I should find it a painful task, to part with my beloved people. Something must be done. I felt perplexed. My good brother-in-law, Mr. Thomas Beckingsale, of Cheltenham called to see us and we laid the matter before him. I told him that Downington House and the land adjoining were about to be sold by auction and that it was said that the property might be bought cheaply; that if I could secure it on moderate terms I would open an academy, and that I thought I might succeed very well. When he knew more of the property, he said,

"If you can buy it at the price you name, it will be cheap, and if it does not answer your purpose, it will be just the place for me to retire to bye and bye. Buy it, by all means, if you can." This was his parting advice. I thought much of it, as he was a man of good judgment and a very sincere friend, one of nature's true nobility. After a few enquiries, I made a bold and honourable bidding, for the beautiful and complete home.[1]

One day, the late George Millward Esq. of Lechlade House, hailed me in the road and asked me respectfully and kindly if it was true, that I was about buying the Downington Estate. I said that I had some thoughts about it.

"Have you examined the roof of the house?" said he, "and is it true that the dry rot is in the boards &c? Would you have any objections to my taking my builder over the property to examine it thoroughly? I have had more experience in these matters than younger people can be expected to have."

"Sir," I replied, "I feel very much obliged to you, and shall be thankful

---

[1] Downington House, Lechlade, was bought 25 December 1835, for £1,110 down, with a mortgage of £600 from a relative of his wife. He sold to James Edwards, of Eastcott, Swindon, 22 July 1854. William Beckinsale of Longborough, a gardener, and James Fidel, of Faringdon, an auctioneer, were also involved in the sale. *(Letter to L. Breeze from A.J. Baxter written on 19 December 1975)*

for any advice you can give me in this matter."

"You call upon me tomorrow morning about nine o'clock," said he, "and I will give you my opinion."

I did so and he gave me a very favourable account of the property; still he doubted the propriety of my purchasing it, till I told him that I intended to open an Academy there.

"If that is your object," he said, "I highly commend it," and he spoke of my character in such respectful terms, saying, he had no doubt of my success. No father could have spoken more kindly to a son, than that gentleman spoke to me about that matter. I at length completed the purchase, which cost me nearly £1200 conveyancing &c. and all.

Several persons felt very surprized at my temerity, as the house was very generally believed to be haunted, and to purchase property under such circumstances appeared to many to be a very unwise act at least, if not one of daring presumption. It was said that a former owner and occupier had been murdered in an upper room and that his body was afterwards dragged down the front stairs and found by the servants in the morning in the entrance hall. A patch of dried blood was shewn me in the room where the dreadful deed was said to have been perpetrated. The day we moved our goods there, I requested the carpenter to remove this red spot with his plane, but he shook his head rather significantly and said,

"Sir, it cannot be done. Murdered blood stains through the whole of the board."

"Never mind," said I, "plane away."

Chip after chip came off, each one a little less stained than the former. Although the man was very unbelieving, he was obliged, at length, to confess that the stain was quite removed without going deep into the board. I have no doubt, that it was no more than a portion of red paint that happened to be spilt from some painter's can, which, through neglect, dried up and that superstitious people would not try to remove it. Many a ghost story had, no doubt, originated and gained an extensive circulation and general credence too, from less probable circumstances, as this house had been occupied by persons of very peculiar and eccentric habits, although, I have no idea that any such dark deeds as those generally reported, have ever taken place in the house.

I have no fear of apparitions. My belief is this, that we have more to fear from the living than from the dead. He that is once buried will be seen no more till the last great day. The above is a very general saying, still I will not undertake to maintain, against the concurrent and unvaried testimony of all ages and all nations, that the dead are seen no more, as the thing may be possible. There is not a people, rude or learned, among whom apparitions of the dead are not related and believed. The opinion, which, perhaps, prevails as far as human nature is diffused, could only become universal by its truth; those who never heard of one another, would not have agreed in a tale, which nothing but experience can make credible. That it is doubted by single cavillers can very little weaken the general evidence, and some who deny it with their tongues, confess it in their fears.

It may well be asked, if I thought it possible for the dead to come again and disturb the peace and order of society, how came I to take up my abode in a haunted house? Well, I believe that the Most High is a God of order and equity; that, as a rule, he will not punish the innocent for the sins of the guilty, and, under the influence of that belief, I took possession of the above premises, an act which I never had any reason to regret.

Having taken possession of the premises and secured the services of a very competent usher in the person of Charles Southall Esquire, a gentleman who had graduated at Pembroke College, Oxford, with the intention of entering the Church, but, having had some conscientious scruples upon the subject, he came and continued with me about six years. The circulars being issued and the scholastic duties fairly began, we continued through the first year and found, before its close, that we had a full school, an abundant cause for encouragement and thankfulness. We had not only a flourishing and promising establishment sprung up into existence in a short time, but the Lechlade Chapel and four other chapels in connection with my ministry, were well attended also, and the fertilizing showers of God's grace descended upon us from day to day, filling our hearts with gladness and our mouths with praises.

My farming business answered my purpose very well. I had two fine cows, none much better in the parish, and good milkers, as the land was rich and productive. The milk was sold by the servant man and I was generally fortunate in getting an honest servant, one that I could trust, who would sell the milk pure and unadulterated, and I have no doubt this was done as he could always get plenty of customers. I had a beautiful pony, a gig and a four wheel carriage also. I found these necessary with my large establishment and ministerial engagements and could not well do without them. I ought to say that my good wife was my right arm, always ready to help me in my work and a first rate manager of everything that came within the sphere of her operations.

We made it a rule to pay ready money for all we had, so that we could command provision of the best quality at moderate charges. We paid annually several hundred pounds in the town and neighbourhood which secured us great respect and gave us very extensive influences. I should not be incorrect, I believe, if I say that the years we spent at Downington House were the most happy and the most useful years we ever spent in this life. Ours was the house of call to all good people, whenever they came and at whatever hour, as we always had plenty to set before them. This no vain boast but the word of truth and soberness, as there are many now living who can bear witness to the truth of the statement.

When we first went to reside at Downington House, we found some difficulty in engaging servants, and when we had them, we had to look after them closely, as they were always on the lookout for the ghost, and often tried to frighten each other. One girl was much given to this. Every now and then she would call out to the other servants, "There he is!" One evening she was well served out for this. In passing by some laurel trees in the garden, she said she heard something so awful that she ran towards the house screaming at the top of her voice; she was so crazy there was no getting near her, and she continued in that state the greater part of the night and was ill for several days after. She had notice to leave after she got better, as it was not safe to keep such a silly girl on the premises. I have no idea that she heard anything more than the rustling of the leaves as she passed by the trees, so that she actually frightened herself into this dangerous state.

I really was alarmed one evening by a statement made by Mr. Southall.

It was this.

"As I stood," said he, "in the back entrance at the little gate, I saw a very tall figure standing in the window of the dining room. It was like a lady with very long features, a downcast and very sorrowful countenance, and with a turban on her head. She could not be less than eight or nine feet high. I kept my eye upon her and made right for the window across the seed beds, as I felt determined to keep the sight and find out what it meant, for I had no doubt it was a supernatural vision, but as I neared the window it vanished all at once and I saw it no more."

Now this was a problem to be solved if possible. I saw that Mr. Southall was sensibly affected by it, but saw no way of clearing up the mystery. I knew that his sympathies were strongly in favour of the supernatural, as he had told me some time previously, that he once saw a very singular apparition near his own town, Northleach. He said he was walking down a lane at night and he suddenly met a huge figure like a man, some three or four yards high. It passed him with a whizzing sound and a gust of wind passed with it, and, as a proof that it was supernatural, he said that his dog was very much frightened and ran to him trembling with his tail down between his legs. Thinking over this tale gave me little relief. It explained nothing, except that the gentleman, learned as he unquestionably was, was a believer in supernatural appearances. Strange thoughts these were to take to bed with you! I went to rest it is true, but not to sleep. Who could sleep with a head so full of ghost stories?

I looked at the tale on one side, then on the other, round about it and all over it, but all remained as dark as night for some hours. Then all at once light broke in upon my mind. The problem seemed solved, the mystery unravelled. I felt amused and pleased. It was this. The previous evening was dry, lovely, and calm as a summer's eve and I had indulged the boys for once, in allowing them to play on the lawn in front of the house. They had played at prison and base and had tied their pocket handkerchiefs round their heads to look like turbans. One must have stood at the prison just before the front window and I guessed it was Master K. as his face would answer the description given. I got up the next morning at the usual time, six o'clock, and found Mr. S. and the boys in the lavatory.

I said, "Master K. Come this way." I placed him at one corner of the ve-randah in front of the house, told him to put on his white turban and look in a certain direction as he did the evening when at play, and to continue to do so till I returned. I then went to the little gate and found my conjec-tures quite correct. There was the vision complete; the tall figure, long vis-age, turban, &c. The floor of the room being lower than the coach road in front, looking through the room by means of the two windows, south and east, brought the head up to the upper panes, hence the illusion. I called Mr. S., he saw it and laughing at himself said,

"I am perfectly satisfied, but if you had not explained it so satisfactorily, I should have believed it to be a ghost to my dying day."

So much for apparitions and I have no doubt that if the various cases named, from time to time were more carefully investigated, we should hear less about these marvellous affairs.

We were blessed with a revival of religion at Lechlade and the other stations, which we used to call our first revival. It came gently upon us, al-most unsought and unlooked for. As a church we were diligent in the use of the means, but not making any unusual or extra effort, yet the gracious shower came, the congregations increased, and the people became deeply impressed with a sense of sin, of their lost condition, and of the need of salvation. I have sometimes had half a dozen persons meet me as I came out of the pulpit, bathed in tears, and crying for mercy, as if in the great-est distress of soul, as much like truly anxious enquirers as ever I saw any persons, and a few of them were some of the most unlikely persons in the town. Our hearts were indeed filled with gladness, as we saw such evident tokens of the Lord's presence among us. I had the pleasure of baptizing thirty willing and rejoicing converts in the space of little more than twelve months, which was to us (in such a place, and among a thin population) a new thing, and it strengthened our hands and our hearts surprizingly. It was evidently the Lord's work and we were well prepared to give him all the praise.

We had what we called our second revival, some few years afterwards, and a delightful season that was, but not equal to the first, although many precious souls were saved and the church quickened to greater life and energy. Poor old shepherd J__ Packer was brought in about this time, with many others; the old man had attended this chapel for above thirty years, without feeling the power of the word till now. He had been a strictly moral man for all those years it is true, yet only a mere formalist, insensible to danger and even dead in trespasses and sins. How marked the change! He became all life, all love, and all zeal. He urged to be baptized immediately, and to become a member of the Church, we said that we should have the ordinance administered shortly, as we expected several more to come forward. Only a few weeks had passed when the good man came to me one Sabbath morning and said with tears,

"Why, Mr. Breeze, I long to be baptized!"

I replied by saying that we should, most likely, be able to attend to it in a week or two.

"Why, Sir," said he, "I may be dead before then."

"Well, friend," I said, "I hope you do not think that you cannot go to heaven unless you are baptized." Now mark the good man's reply! It is worth recording and worthy of attention.

"No, Sir, I do not think that baptism will save me, but I feel that I shall be better satisfied to meet my dear Saviour after I have obeyed him in this sacred ordinance."

"Friend," I said, "I am glad to find you have such correct views of this sacred rite and I will see to it that you shall soon have the pleasure of obeying the commands of your Redeemer."

It was to him not salvation, but the answer of a good conscience towards God. The next Sabbath was to the aged convert and several others baptized at the same time, a day of much gladness, never to be forgotten. "To obey is better than sacrifice".

At another time when we were about having a baptizing there was a young servant girl out of a situation at the time, staying with a woman named Jane S__, a good sort of woman in her way, but careless about her soul's salvation, so much so that she refused to receive the religious tracts offered her, and even treated the persons who called with them with rudeness. These two females hearing about the baptizing amused themselves very much about it. They would go to the dipping, yes, that they would, even if they went there on their hands and knees. This, bye the bye, would have been an undertaking for them as the ordinance was to be administered at the new chapel at Filkins, about four miles from Lechlade. It appears that just as they were ready for the journey, and while talking sportively and irreverently about the ordinance, the poor young woman was seized with paralysis, and a very severe attack it was. This solemn visitation was very much felt by us all, and many an earnest prayer was offered up to God that evening on behalf of the sufferer, that He would mercifully convert what appeared to be marks of the Divine displeasure into a blessing, and that this awful dispensation might work for her good.

We have reason to believe that it was so in this case. Many in the place heard the sad news with feelings of horror and others said they hoped it would be a warning to thoughtless ones, who were accustomed to speak irreverently and profanely about sacred things. The Revd E. L. Bennett, the vicar of the parish, a gentleman whom I always much respected, hearing the report called upon the young woman, and finding her in an awfully stricken state, told her that it was a mercy for her that her life was spared at all, and that it was a wonder that God did not strike her dead upon the spot for reviling his holy institutions; that the Baptists were perfectly right in what they did; that dipping was in accordance with the *Book of Common Prayer*, and in harmony with the baptism of Jesus Christ in the River Jordan.

I have every reason to believe that God did overrule the sad visit for the good of the young woman. As soon as she was able to get to our chapel, she came, and no one who attended there seemed to be more attentive, more feeling, or more devout than she. She was at length removed from us to the union workhouse at Faringdon, when we, in a measure, lost sight of her. As to the other woman, Jane S__, she became one of the best of women, she soon after became a member of the Church and continued to adorn her profession till the day of her happy and peaceful death. Some years before the good woman's departure, she underwent a painful surgical operation, which she bore with surprizing patience and Christian fortitude, to the surprise of all present. The deep impression of each was that God, in love, gave the dear woman unusual strength for the occasion.

His faithful word declares to thee
That as thy day, thy strength shall be.

Whilst I was in London at one time, I received a letter from my good
wife stating, among other things, that the Primitive Methodists had held
a service in the Market Place at Lechlade, that the people served them
very roughly, and that she tried to interfere in favour of peace and order;
but what can a female do, even the best and most influential among them,
with a number of roughs? However she did the best she could and came
in for some of the honours conferred on the rest, even a potato shot or
two from the hands of the mob. The preacher came again the next week,
took up his stand as before and the baser sort, the low fellows of the town,
were assembled in considerable strength fully bent upon mischief. It was
a very uproarious, noisy and shameful affair. At the close of the meeting
one fellow went up to the minister and threw a bucket of filthy water upon
him and swore that if he ever came there again, he would hang him up
by the neck. This had been the sad state of things when I returned, and
I felt ashamed and mortified that I lived in a town containing so many
rude savages in human form, and, that in Christian England and in the
19th century. I felt determined to put a stop to it, cost what it might. The
next evening came, I was prepared to receive them, having been informed
that immense preparations had been made in the shape of eggs, potatoes,
a large leather tube filled with blood, &c. I was there and the constable,
Mr. Tovey, a very civil man, and a man who would do all in his power to
promote my wishes, stood by my side to the great disappointment of the
blacks and those who came expecting an evening's row. I may say also, to
the joy of all who loved peace and order [that] while ready and on the lookout for the minister, we saw a party come along Oak Street from the Little
Faringdon Road singing like dauntless heroes as if they felt that victory was
theirs even before they had entered upon the evening's conflict.

"Well done," I said to the constable, "let us be firm and brave also,"

When the party came opposite to the place where we stood, I called out
to the minister,

"Friend, please to hold your service on that green under the shelter of that wall and the constable and I will see you protected."

He replied, "Thank you, Sir," and entered upon the service. All continued peaceful till about the middle of the service, when I saw a fellow come up that fine wide street, well charged with brown stout and bellowing, like a savage bull.

"Mind," I whispered to the constable, "this is the signal for the battle." I stepped out a few paces from the wall and said,

"Constable, take charge of that man."

The officer did the thing very nicely. He walked gently to meet the fellow, there was no bluster made nor any official importance shown, but he merely whispered a few kind, firm words to the man, that settled the matter in an instant. The man became sober, quiet, and harmless as a lamb all at once, the service ceased peacefully and the congregation left the place in an orderly manner. The constable attended with me the next week, when all was quiet and peaceful, altho' it had been freely reported that there would be a serious riot. We also were present on the third week, but no disturbance was attempted till nearly the close of the service, when a few young men, the sons of farmers of an adjoining parish came, thinking, I suppose, that they could intimidate us and drive us from our purpose. I saw them come and walked off to meet them, intending to speak to them some kind words of advice, as you can generally reason with people of education and thereby prevent impending evils. When I drew near them, they all at once turned round and went back [at a] full run, feeling, perhaps, that they had a bad cause on hand and that the sooner they gave it up the better. One thing amused us much. These young men brought with them a horn, intending, very likely, to give us a little music, but their retreat was so sudden that they did not use it except by merely blowing, "boo, boo, boo." as they ran away. It may have been their retreat notes, I cannot say, as I never troubled myself to enquire further into the matter.

This was the last battle out of the many I have had with low, petty, contemptible persecutors. The following lines are worth insertion.

> Tender handed touch the nettle
> And it stings you for your pains,

Grasp it like a man of mettle
And it soft as silk remains.
So it is with vulgar natures,
Use them gently, they repel.
Press them hard like nutmeg graters
And the rogues will serve you well.

My respected neighbour, the Vicar of this parish, who had ministered in the Church full twenty years, had a valuable living presented to him in Lincolnshire, so he left the town to the regret of many, for the gentleman was deservedly respected. He married his second wife at the same time and he and his bride passed through the town on the day of the wedding. Great respect was shewn them by the good people of the town, by erecting triumphal arches, hoisting flags, &c. The gentleman also showed some little courtesy to me on leaving, by sending me a kind note apologizing for not calling to take his leave of me and enclosing a large piece of wedding cake. I met a gentleman lately, an old friend of Mr. Bennett at one of our stations, who said that the Church and the Chapel at Lechlade sustained a great loss when Mr. Bennett and Mr. Breeze left the town and that the loss had not then been made up.

Some four years after I came to Lechlade, my late beloved pastor, the Revd John Jones of Newtown, departed this life. If I remember aright, the dear man had for several years a little pimple on the back of one of his hands, which he thought but little about. It by degrees became more and greatly inflamed and at last he had to tie it up in a sling. However it became more serious and proved to be a cancer, so that something had to be done to try to correct the evil, and that without delay. It was at last decided that the beloved sufferer should go to Shrewsbury and place himself under the charge of an eminent physician there, in hopes of receiving some substantial benefit. He went hopefully, accompanied with the sympathies and prayers of his people, and I may say, of the whole town and neighbourhood. The good man was so much beloved and respected by all who knew him, and all felt they had a friend whose valuable life was in danger. He had not been at Shrewsbury long before it was fully ascertained that nothing could save his life but amputation. This, after great anxiety, much deliberation and earnest prayer to God for direction, was decided on. The dear sufferer passed through the painful surgical operation with great patience and fortitude, and all appeared for a time to be fair and promising, to the great joy of his anxious family and all his friends. The following morning, or soon after, the patient observed his medical attendants in deep and solemn consultation and suspected the cause of it. He at length said,

"Gentlemen, if you have a secret to reveal, withhold it not from me as I have nothing to fear."

The sad information was given, that in so many hours the fatal disease would reach the vital parts and terminate his earthly existence. He received the awful tidings with great composure of mind and said,

"I should like to preach one more sermon before I die."

Preaching the glorious Gospel had been for many years his happy and beloved work, and he evidently felt the ruling passion strong in death. At a convenient hour, the favour was granted him and he did, no doubt, preach as a dying man to dying men, as it had always been the custom of this faithful minister of Jesus Christ. At length the solemn hour of release came and the happy spirit entered upon its eternal rest in the year 1831 and in the forty-ninth year of his age. It may be said of him, that he did the work of a long life in a short time, but he would have been the last of men to say so, or to exalt the creature, as he always had such humble views of his own endeavours to serve his great and good Master. The funeral procession left Shrewsbury at an early hour on the day of interment and on arriving at Welshpool on the journey to Newtown, they saw in the streets, thousands of its sympathizing inhabitants to whom the dear departed minister had been well known.

The Revd B. Kent of Shrewsbury addressed the multitude in the street upon solemn subjects, suitable to the mournful occasion, and afterwards they resumed their slow and sorrowful journey. Within about two miles of Newtown they met one of the most sad and sorrowful processions ever witnessed in that part of the country, headed by two of the county magistrates and many of the more respectable inhabitants on horseback, together with thousands of pedestrians from the town and neighbourhood, who came and wept at the sorrowful sight. A friend of mine, giving an account of it said that the thousands who came literally bedewed the road with their tears. Arriving at the town where all work had been suspended, the factories all silent, shops closed, and nearly all the people in the streets, all felt, not only that a great man was fallen in Israel, but that each one had lost a father and a friend. Having halted for some little time, when a brief religious service was held in the street, they moved onward to the cemetery at Rhy-d-felen, where the remains of the good man were interred, buried indeed, "In sure and certain hope of a resurrection unto eternal life," amid the sighs and tears of the crowds of mourning people.

The Revd David Phillips also, who had for some years been co-pastor with Mr. Jones, died some time before him. He was on a tour through South Wales and was taken ill in the street at Swansea. He went into a friend's house and said he felt very unwell and that he thought his sickness was unto death, but, said he, "What a mercy to be prepared!" He was one of the most cheerful Christians I ever knew and a very useful preacher of the Gospel in which he was engaged more or less for fifty years. His was cheerfulness without levity, his jokes and wit had nothing of profanity in them, but tended rather to shew that "Religion never was designed to make our pleasures less."

My early association with these servants of Jesus Christ has proved one of the greatest blessings that God has ever conferred upon me, as I never seem to have lost their society. Their presence has always appeared to be with me all through the pilgrimage of life. In solitude and in public, in joy and in sorrow, their loving spirits at all times seem to be at my side to help me on through the weary way, and the happy assurance of meeting at last, with them, and so many other kindred spirits in the kingdom of our Heavenly Father, gives additional brightness to the prospect, and vigour to my drooping spirits.

Having spent nearly twelve years at Downington House engaged in my scholastic and ministerial duties combined, and also having accomplished, in a measure, the education of my sons, my wife had found her position a laborious one and mine had not been less arduous, we began to sigh and wish for a change. One day we saw an advertisement in the papers, "A school wanted, a good home &c." I answered it and soon after a gentleman came down to see us. It was the Revd C. Crump, a highly respectable man and an Independent minister. He had for the ten previous years been chaplain of Mill Hill Grammar School near London. The home and the conditions proposed met his approbation, so we soon came to fair terms and a full understanding. The dear boys in the school became very sensibly affected when they heard of the contemplated change. They wept excessively, so that there was no work done that day. The neighbours felt surprized [for] they naturally supposed that, having such a comfortable home, we had settled down for life, and none of them wished us to leave. The Revd Evanson, Vicar of Inglesham, hearing of it, came over to enquire if it were true. I replied that it was and that the matter was finally settled.

"I am very sorry for it," he said, "as I think you are not doing the thing that is right, and I have come on purpose to try to persuade you not to leave, but, if I am too late, it cannot be helped. I and my friend were talking about it yesterday," he said, referring to Geo. Millward Esq., Captain Coles, and other gentlemen in the neighbourhood, "and we expressed it as our opinion that you were doing well and that there was not a man in the locality more respected by all persons than you were, by rich and poor and by all denominations alike. Also that we were personally sorry at your leaving and hoped you would think better of it, for, be assured of this, Sir, that wherever you go, it will take you 7 or 8 years, at least, to rise among a fresh people to that point of elevation you have attained among us, if indeed you ever do."

"Dear Sir," I said in reply, "I feel truly unworthy of the kind sentiments you express, as regards myself, still I am very sensible of your kindness in thus calling to give expression to the kind feelings of yourself and your friends towards me. Such an act of courtesy and kind neighbourly feeling, I shall not forget to my dying day. As regards my personal position, I am thankful in being able to say that my circumstances are somewhat better now than when I came here and that I shall be able to leave the town creditably, but as to the future all is dark and uncertain." After a little further conversation the kind gentleman left with many expressions of similar kindness, &c.

As far as I can ascertain this was only a specimen of the kind feeling generally entertained towards me by the clergy, the gentry, and the neighbours in general. I name these things not by way of boasting, but as matters of fact, which I think I owe to my family and friends to record, and to the grace of God more especially; to which I am alone indebted for every good and perfect gift.

The next weighty matter I had to attend to, was to resign my pastoral charge. This I found to be a painful task and it cost me and the good people many tears. I had the pleasure of recommending as my successor to the church and congregation my esteemed friend, Mr. Andrew Walsh, who had laboured faithfully with me in the word and doctrine, with considerable acceptance, for several years, and the church very cheerfully and unanimously invited him to succeed me in the office of pastor.

It soon became known to the various Baptist churches for some distance, that I was at liberty to take a fresh charge, when I soon heard of two churches who would like to secure my services, but as I had still the charge of the little church at Stratton, near Swindon, we decided to remove there for the present.

We left Lechlade, a kind people, and a lovely home, not with the most cheerful feelings, as we really had doubts in our minds, whether we were doing the thing that was right or not. When we reached Stratton, all seemed dark and forbidding, yet we lived to see that it was right, and that our heavenly Father led us by a way that we knew not, and that it is not in man that liveth to direct his steps.

14

Stratton, New Town & Swindon, 1847

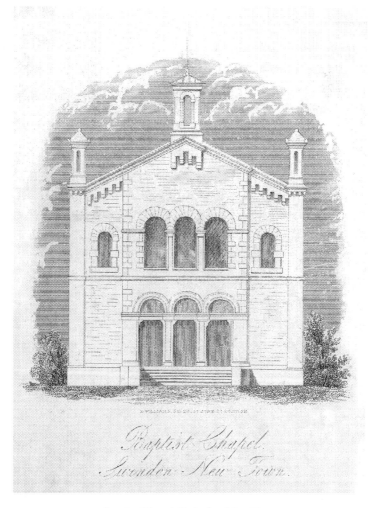

Baptist Chapel, Swindon New Town

Some Extracts from the Church Book of Stratton Baptist Chapel:

"In the year of our Lord 1750 and in the 24th year of the reign of George the 2nd, king of G[t] Britain, France and Ireland, a few pious Baptists agreed to build a chapel at Stratton S[t] Margaret, for the worship of God in that place and for the use, more especially, of the Baptist denominations forever. This was the first dissenting place of worship erected in this locality and several persons came time after time to worship God in this little sanctuary. To the praise of the good people meeting there, be it said that all who loved Jesus Christ of whatever persuasion, met with a cordial welcome, to unite with them in Christian fellowship, in breaking of bread and in prayer. The test for communion was then, and has been ever since, love to the Redeemer, a belief in the great truths of the Christian religion, and a life corresponding with the sacred precepts of the Holy Bible. Those were times of great moral darkness and of constant harassing persecution. The good man who preached the gospel, and the people who came to hear endured a great fight of affliction, for often when assembled, the mob has surrounded the chapel, split the doors open, broken the windows and shamefully abused the people who had quietly met together for divine worship. That was indeed the reign of terror and of cruelty; bull baiting, badger baiting, cockfighting, backsword exercise, and field sport on the Holy Sabbath, was the order of the day and woe to the man or woman, who had the temerity to say a word against these immoral practices. The established Church stood alone in her glory, and her clergy, almost to a man, most heartily promoted the above wicked habits of the times in which they lived. The moral state of Swindon, about a century ago, may be seen from the following sad statements."

Extract from the Journal of Mr. John Cennick[1], the Evangelist of North Wiltshire, the sweet Christian Poet of the Day – 1740

---

[1] John Cennick, 1718-1755, was brought up an Anglican, and originally became a follower of John Wesley. He later parted company with Wesley and began his evangelistic campaign which brought him into close touch with the Moravian Brethren. The attack at Stratton was one of many he faced. He wrote simple manuals of instruction for the religious education of his followers. He left his societies in the care of the Brethren, then went to Germany where he was received as a Moravian. When he returned, he began his campaign in Ireland. [From *The Moravian Church* / J.E. Hutton, Chapter XI, "The Labours of John Cennick, 1739-1755.

"Brother Howell Harris, of Wales, came to see me in Wiltshire, and on Tuesday, the 23 June, 1740, with about 24 on horses, he accompanied me to Swindon, about ten miles from Brinkworth, and not far from the Vale of the White Horse, where I had appointed to preach. We found a large company assembled in the Grove, with whom I sang and prayed, but was hindered from preaching by a great mob, who made a noise and played in the midst of the people, and then with guns they fired over our heads, holding the muzzles of their pieces so near our faces that we were both made as black as tinkers with the powder. We were not affrighted, but opened our breasts, telling them we were ready to lay down our lives for our doctrine, and had nothing to say against it, even if those guns were levelled at our hearts. They then got the dust out of the highway and covered us all over, and then played an engine upon us, which they filled out of the stinking ditches, till we were just like men in the pillory. While they played upon brother Harris spoke to the congregation, and when they turned the engine upon me, then he preached and this continued till they had spoiled the engine and then they threw whole buckets of water and mud upon us. When we had stood in this manner more than an hour, a spectacle of the utmost shame before many weeping people, and before the whole mob, we were led up to the town to Mr. Lawrence's house, who had invited us thither, where we borrowed some old things to change and came back to Brinkworth. This persecution was carried on by Mr. Goddard[2], a leading gentleman of that place, who lent the mob his guns, halberd and engine, and bade them to use us as badly as they could, only not to kill us and he himself sat on horseback the whole time, laughing to see us so treated. After we had left the town, they dressed up two images, and called one Cennick and the other Harris, and then burnt them. Also the next day after we had been there, they rose about the house of Mr. Lawrence and broke all his windows and with stones cut and wounded four of his family, and knocked down one of his daughters, and so left them for the day, but if they heard them singing hymns, or supposed a minister to be there, they continued

---

[2] Apparently the lord of the manor, Pleydell Goddard. [*The Victoria History of the Counties of England, A History of Wiltshire, Vol. 9, p. 151-152.*]

to riot about the houses. Some few days afterwards, the mob again got to-gether, resolving to pull down Mr. Lawrence's house, but, as soon as they began, there fell such a violent shower of rain as obliged them to disperse. It was also remarkable, that about this time an uncommon clap of thunder was heard over the town, which sadly terrified the inhabitants. In this storm an oak tree, which stood in a field of Mr. Goddard's, was split into the finest splinters and scattered all over the field. This seemed to portend something bad, and was generally observed, when people saw what followed.

"I had appointed some time after this, to preach at Stratton, a place not more than two miles from Swindon, at which time, (as was supposed be-cause in my addresses to the people, I made frequent mention of the blood of Christ) the chief person concerned in the former riot, got a butcher to save all the blood he could, in order that they might play it out of the en-gine upon us, and so give us blood enough. But before I went to Stratton, God struck with particular judgments all the authors of this design at once. John and Thomas Villett Esquires, the parson of Stratton, and Silvester Kean, a bailiff, all bled at the nose and some at the mouth without ceas-ing, till one of the former fell into dead fits and could not any more be trusted alone. Neither did the minister recover, for it brought him also to his grave. As for S. Kean, he continued to bleed at times, at such an ex-travagant rate, that it threw him into a deep decay, in which he lingered ten days without having any one to visit him because he stank alive, and, on the 31st March following, he died cursing terribly. On Saturday 6th of September, after I had preached at Brinkworth School, or meeting, about fifty persons, on horses and as many on foot, went with me to Stratton, where we had appointed a meeting for the day. On the road I opened my New Testament on those words, "We are persecuted but not forsaken," which served to hint to me what would happen. However we had many people and a lovely meeting. But before I had said much, came the mob again, from Swindon, with swords, staves and poles. Without respect to age or sex, they knocked down all who stood in their way, so that some had the blood streaming down their faces, and others were taken up al-most beaten and trampled to death. Many of our dear friends were cut and bruised sadly, and I got many severe blows myself. We got away into a Baptist meeting house just by, where I spoke to a house full in much affection, and took leave. When we were again mounted, we thanked God, who had counted us worthy to suffer thus for His Gospel's sake, and then made towards Lyneham thinking that now our enemies had fully revenged themselves upon us. But we soon found to the contrary, for presently they overtook us and beat us barbarously. Our horses were so startled, that it was a real mercy we had not been killed, or did not kill others, who were on foot, for we rode through the midst of the people, our persecutors whipping the horses with all their might, while the people on foot, to save themselves, rushed into the hedges and ditches, and hid themselves where they could. At last we came into a part of our road where were many gates across the track, where they posted themselves, and beat inhumanly each of us as we rode by. This they did for about two miles, when a countryman shewed us a narrow lane, which led into another road, by which we escaped further hurt, our enemies (unaware of our change of route) riding before, into a strait place, expecting we should come that way. In this hurry several lost their hats and handkerchiefs, and some with difficulty saved their lives. After we had left the first road, and were a little still and collected, we could hear behind us most dreadful crying, for our friends on foot were being pursued and used equally ill as ourselves. Several of them came home so bruised and hurt, as is not easily to be believed. One, James Cottle of Stanton, who had been unmercifully beaten, seeing one that had beaten him, fall down by means of a large thorn which ran deep into his foot, stopped, and meekly helped him to get it out, and this act so moved the man that he left off beating, and turned back with the rest of his companions. As soon as we came to Lyneham, we were welcomed back with many tears by some hundreds of people, who had heard we were killed; for those who had made haste before reported that they had heard the mob swear that they would butcher us. When I came to brother Bryant's door, I kneeled down and thanked the Lord with my company, that he had saved us this day. I preached and took leave of them all and the next morning set out for London, though my shoulders remained black with blows for three weeks afterwards.

Now, Mr. Goddard rejoiced that he had given us enough, but not many days passed ere, as he was riding the same horse on which he sat laughing to see us abused at Swindon, a servant of his was cleaning the guns which had been fouled in firing at us, and, letting one of them off just as his master rode into the court, the horse started and threw him off, by which means, R. Goddard received some inward hurt, either from the saddle or from the fall, which in a little time caused his death. Some of Swindon affirm that he received his first hurt while he looked on to see us abused, and that the fall which he afterwards got from the horse, merely hastened his end, for he left the world about a fortnight afterwards, raving with pain, aged about 50 years. As he died without making a will, his relatives did not know who should be his heir, and he was left unburied, till the stench of his corpse saw intolerable, and at last he was interred at night privately. Silvester Kean, as was before said, bled to such an unnatural degree, that all his bowels corrupted, and so he miserably ended his life, even cursing himself, and those who encouraged him to meddle with us. This was on the last day of March. Charles Gay, a tailor, one of the chief of the mob and who in particular threatened to butcher us, as well as Thomas Perry, a breeches maker, were together tried for their lives at the assizes for stealing ten guineas, and hardly escaped the gallows. Thomas Looker, a soap boiler, and Thomas Holliday, a labourer, were soon after publicly whipped at Devizes, for stealing fowls. Francis Gay, a brandy seller, Edward Golding, Edward Archer, a mason, Henry Hoddam, a shoemaker, and Thomas Humphreys, a glazier, ran away, some for buying stolen goods and some for debt. Another went beside himself and left the town in deepest melancholy. All this happening, so soon after they persecuted us stopped all further troubles of this kind and made all men afraid to interrupt us in these parts."[3]

An Extract from the "Berkshire Times" giving an account of the ordination of my successor, the Reverend I. Murphy, will tell us a little about successful results.

---

[3] Nonconformity in Swindon during the 18th century seems to have withered after this persecution. A house was licensed as a meeting place for protestant dissenters in 1745, but the extent of its use is unknown. For the rest of the century, the only permanent meeting-place for Swindon nonconformists was the Baptist chapel in Stratton Green. [*V.H.C.W., Swindon*]

"Before entering upon a narrative of the proceedings, it may not be out of place to mention a few facts in connection with the history of this church, as its rise and progress, are so closely connected with the incidents, which have converted New Swindon, from a large tract of land into a populous and flourishing town. In the year 1844, the Revd Richard Breeze, having at that time the charge of a Baptist Church at Lechlade, and also one at Stratton, Swindon, visited Swindon and went to see the New Town, which was just then attracting much attention, in consequence of the transformation which the Great Western Company's Works had effected in the place. There was then no place of worship in New Swindon, the present St Mark's Church being at that time in course of erection. The only place was the parish Church of Old Swindon, which was very small, and then standing on the old site adjoining the grounds of Mr. A. L. Goddard M.P. together with three dissenting chapels. A population made up of persons from all parts, like the artizans at New Swindon, naturally contained many dissenters, and a wish was expressed on their part that they should have a chapel. Mr. Breeze remarked to those who spoke to him, that he wished it was in his power to meet their wants, but there was no prospect of doing so at the present. In 1847, Mr. Breeze resigned the pastorate at Lechlade, with the intention of leaving the neighbourhood. Several persons, however, urged upon him to endeavour to establish a Baptist Church in New Swindon, and a committee was formed with that object. Some £300 was subscribed which amount, however, was almost absorbed by the purchase of the land and the cost of other preliminaries. Having obtained a site, Mr. Breeze felt anxious to begin to build; but was unable to prevail upon any of the committee to undertake the joint responsibility of meeting the payments to the contractor. Nothing daunted, he resolved to undertake the responsibility himself. Sir Morton (then Mr.) Peto, gave a liberal subscription and one of the gentlemen of his engineering staff provided the plans, which Sir Morton generously presented to the committee. The foundation stone was laid by the Rev^d Dr. Cox, L.L.D. of Hackney, and on the 4th January, 1849, the edifice was opened for divine worship. The Revd Jas. Sherman, of Surrey Chapel (the predecessor of the eloquent Mr. Newman Hall), the Revd Howard Hinton, and the Revd T. Winter of Bristol, conducting the opening services. The Revd R. Breeze was appointed minister by the trustees, and, on the establishment of a church, he was formally appointed to the pastorate. The fortunes of the cause were varying, the great success which followed the opening of the building, having been checked by the contemplated removal of the Great Western Works from Swindon, the number of hands (1700) employed at the establishment, being reduced to about 500. This was followed by a period of great depression in Swindon, in which all interests suffered. With the determination of the Company to continue their works at Swindon, came a revival of prosperity, and a fresh influx of population. The Baptist Church, in common with other places of worship, gradually filled and a numerous congregation and a largely attended Sunday School continued. In the beginning of 1865, the Revd R. Breeze retired from ill health, a protracted and painful illness having greatly enfeebled him."

Extract from the "Swindon Advertiser"

"There is something interesting in the history of the Baptist Church at New Swindon, more especially from its connection with the Baptist Chapel at Stratton, the mother chapel of dissent in this neighbourhood, a chapel built at a time when dissent was neither safe nor respectable. The ecclesiastical District of St Marks was formed, and St Mark's Church was erected and endowed by the Great Western Railway Company. But with the new men there came new thoughts and new ideas, and many had to grope their way through the mud to such places of dissenting worship as the Old Town possessed. At this time, 1844, the Revd R. Breeze, who for fifteen years had been occupying the pulpit at Stratton, in conjunction with his pastorate at Lechlade, visited New Swindon and availed himself of the opportunity afforded by the distribution of religious tracts, to consult with the people as to the erection of a Baptist place of worship, many of the newcomers having been in the habit of attending dissenting places of worship, before they came here, so that Mr. Breeze's suggestion was most warmly received. It was not, however, till 1847, that Mr. Breeze saw his way clearly to the erection of a chapel at this new railway town; however, in the course of that year he determined on leaving Lechlade and devoting his attention to Stratton and New Swindon. A committee of persons favourable to the erection of a chapel at the latter place was formed, and in a short time a sum of £300 was secured for that purpose. The price of land was at this time so great, that it absorbed the above sum in purchasing a suitable site for that purpose. There were however some willing workmen, and the scheme was not allowed to fall through, and Mr. Breeze was soon rewarded for his labours in getting together subscriptions and by seeing the work fairly started. Sir Morton Peto, the present M.P. for Bristol [1865-1868], in addition to a handsome subscription, gave the plans for the new building free of all cost. The foundation stone of the new edifice was laid in the summer of 1848 by the Rev^d Dr. Cox of Hackney and the chapel was opened on the 4th January, 1849, by the Revd James Sherman and the Revd Howard Hinton, both of London, and the Revd T. Winter of Bristol, the Revd R. Breeze being appointed to the pastorate. From this period downward, the history of New Swindon has been a most chequered one. At one period the extensive engineering shops of the Great Western Railway, have been filled with workmen engaged day and night with everything around partaking of that bustle and activity that was to be seen within. At other times nothing but stagnation, the hands reduced in number and those who were left working at short time, workshops have been closed, and the machinery put away in fallow.

"In the early part of 1865, Mr. Breeze, who had during the greater part of the past year suffered from a very severe illness, retired from the New Swindon pulpit, the duties attending the Stratton and the New Swindon Chapels being more than he could attend to. From this time there was no fixed minister at New Swindon, the pulpit being supplied by various ministers. At length the Revd I. M. Murphy, a student from the Revd C. H. Spurgeons college received, and accepted, an invitation to the pastorate. Since Mr. Murphy's acceptance of the New Swindon pulpit, the success inaugurated by Mr. Breeze has been well continued, and this with the growing population, has rendered an enlargement of the premises very desirable, &c., &c."

N. B. These extracts are the voice of the public press, and as general statements they are not far from correct.

Continuation of Extract from the Church Book of Stratton Baptist Chapel

"It appears that the above chapel was supplied by various ministers for some years, and that the first settled pastor was the Revd I. Holmes, who was also Pastor of the Baptist Church, Kingston Lisle, Berks., supplying each chapel alternate Sabbaths. He was said to be a very good man and much respected. At his decease the Revd I. Smith succeeded to the pastorate of the two churches united, a good man and full of the Holy Ghost, as some aged persons still living can testify. The Revd D. Williams Junr of Fairford, became pastor of both churches on the decease of Mr. Smith. He was a good man and was much beloved by all who knew him. Mr. Williams died in the year 1829, having taken a severe cold, in returning through the rain from Stratton on Sabbath evening. The Revd R. Breeze, pastor of the Baptist Church, Lechlade, received an invitation from the church and congregation at Stratton, to take the charge over them in conjunction with his charge at Lechlade, and being urged by the Trustees of the late Abram Atkins Esq., he consented to do so and has continued his services there to the present time. In the year 1844, Mr. Breeze and a friend of his, went to visit New Swindon for the first time, taking with them a bundle of tracts. There was no place of worship in the town, then containing about 1500 persons, the present St Mark's Church being in the course of erection, and to get up to Swindon to worship, during the greater part of the year, they would have to pass through dirt and water of considerable depth. In visiting these interesting and intelligent families, Mr. Breeze found that a large majority had been accustomed to attend dissenting places of worship. They warmly expressed a wish that a chapel were built there, as well as a church. So this Mr. Breeze replied that he wished it was in his power to help them in this matter, but did not then see the least probability of doing so himself."

I shall now, in as brief a space as I can, give a simple and truthful statement of plain matters of fact, as they occurred.

I did visit the New Town in 1844 as stated, and was considerably affected by the morally destitute condition of those interesting young people; there was scarcely a person of years among them; but as to building a chapel for their accommodation, I saw no probability of it at the time. I often thought of the visit and regretted that something could not be done for the people.

When I left Lechlade for Stratton, it was not at all with the intention of extending my efforts to New Swindon. I went there, merely with the view of spending three or four months, to seek direction from above, and prayerfully to deliberate as to what steps I should take in the future, so that my movements might not be characterized with rashness, or undue haste. I had received communications from two churches, who each of them wished to secure my services, and I knew not which to accept, in case a direct invitation to the pastorate came from either. I visited them both, and found that the good people at each place very heartily wished me to settle among them. I found that I had to make my own election.

While these matters were pending, the good people at Stratton, Swindon, and the New Town, urged me to make an effort to originate a Baptist interest at this last place, and thereby to extend the old mother church Baptist principles to the New Town. They said that I was the very man for such an undertaking and that this above all others was the time for it, and some said that God had brought me into the neighbourhood for this purpose.

These statements made considerable impression on my mind, as I knew that I had come ever to Stratton contrary to my own plans and my own wishes. I began seriously to think that the hand of the Lord was in it. I began to enquire more into the matter, and before taking any decisive step, I went to Oxford, Abingdon, Reading and London, to seek the advice of ministers and some of the principal friends of the Denomination. When I returned, I went to Melksham, Ironbridge, Bath and Bristol, on the same errand. All the good people urged me much, to go on with the work without any hesitation, and said that they would do all they could to help me through it. To their credit, be it said that they were, as far as I can recollect, with an exception or two, as good as their word. I am not the man to condemn a whole body of true and loving people, simply because some one or two persons may not have proved true.

I felt, by this time, strongly disposed to take the onward step; it was taken; however, and as a dear friend said to me the other day, if ever I took a wrong step in my life it was then. However, it was taken and I would not retreat for the world, were it in my power to do so, altho' I have had some very painful things to pass through on account of it.

A committee of management was formed, the land was paid for, and properly invested in the hands of Trustees, for the use of the Baptist Denomination for ever. I wrote to the two churches, who were waiting for my reply, to inform them of the decision, to which I had come, and went on with all speed to collect funds for the erection of the new Chapel. While thus engaged, the Great Western Railway Company became embarrassed, several hundred hands were rather suddenly discharged, and strange reports were made, that the works would be removed from the place, and that the best days of Swindon had passed away never to return, &c. After a time, a more favourable view of things was taken and we became a little more hopeful, but not so the committee, they were quite shaken in their confidence. One evening when assembled for business, they all freely expressed an opinion that as the state of things was so unsettled at the New Town, we had better give up all thoughts of building for the present, that in a year or two things might be different. One said that the land might be fenced in, and thus abide till a more promising time. I said I could not possibly agree to that, as I had collected nearly £400 and had pledged my word to many of the kind subscribers, that a chapel should be built, and that I could not allow the thing to stand over in that way. Another said that the Wesleyans were about building a wooden chapel, and had not we better do something of that sort, if we did anything at present. I said that that would not do. I had consulted a builder upon that subject, and he had said that a structure of that kind would cost £400 or £450 and be nothing after all but waste of money.

"If," I said, "we put up anything short of a complete building, let it be a substantial shell, or outside walls, and let us finish it at our leisure." [I said that] I had known that done in one or two cases. After a little more conversation of the same kind, they gave me fully to understand that they did not intend becoming personally responsible to the builder, or any one else, but if I went on with the work in any way I thought best, they would do what they could to help me on with the undertaking. To do the good people credit I am happy to say that they gave me much of their sympathy and assistance, but, not equal to what I had expected, as they were gentlemen in good circumstances.

Well, when I came out of the room that night, I felt very sad, and was glad to breathe the fresh air again; my son William was with me, a lad of sixteen, who, when he found himself at large burst into tears, his pent up sorrow flowed out freely, and I found it convenient to have my handkerchief at hand to keep my own cheeks dry. We had a tale of sorrow to unfold when we got home, and a bitter night we had, but I believe it did us good. I have no doubt it led us to cease from man and to put our trust more fully in God the faithful and unchanging Friend.

To give up the project like a fainthearted coward, I could not, I dared not. I went forth alone and singlehanded and God went with me, and gave me favour in the eyes of the people.

The Independent and the Baptist ministers really surprised me with their kindness. Almost to a man they opened their pulpits to me and allowed me to appeal to their people. The Wesleyan and Primitive Methodists treated me courteously, but having to work hard to support their own Institutions, they could not do much for me. The kind members of the Episcopal Church, cheerfully gave me scores of pounds and the good Quakers, or Friends, very kindly replied to my appeals. As already stated, the plans for the chapel were gratuitously given, and taking shares in a Building Fund in London, I soon found myself in a position to come to terms with the builder.

The noble Chapel, of which I felt justly proud, was much admired by all men of taste and judgment, and was opened for divine worship on the 4th January, 1849. Mine were tears of joy and gratitude to God that day. It was He and He alone who helped me to rise above my troubles and blessed be His holy name.

The gentleman who drew the plans for the chapel said that the ground floor would accommodate 350 persons. Some time after this we wanted more room, and Mr. Sam¹ Spires and Mr. Stephen Fillness, two of our friends kindly undertook, to get money enough to put up a front gallery. They nobly succeeded and the good work was done and paid for. Then came on our second railway panic and this was an awful one. The hands were reduced from some 1800 to 500 or so, and the few retained were put on halftime. Hundreds, or thousands, of the people had to leave, more than half the houses became empty, fearful desolations there were, indeed, and painful to witness.

After this we had a revival, and then, I think it was, we built our vestries and school room.

The third panic came on and the last, but it was not so severe as the former ones. It passed off soon, and from that period, to this, we have seen better days. May they very long continue!

A person said to me lately that Swindon had seen its best days.

I replied, "No, it has better days to come yet. I believe it is destined to become the largest and the most flourishing town in the County of Wiltshire and that before the children of Swindon die of old age."

It was my custom on returning after an absence of a week or two collecting, to call upon the Secretary to enter the proceeds in a book, deducting my expenses, &c. In looking over my books I feel perfectly surprised at my own success. The books being audited just before the opening of the Chapel we had the following pleasing results:

Collected by Mr Breeze	*£1,067 11/-*
Expended, &c	*£1,077 15/5*
20th December 1849	
Examined and found}	*J. B. Jordan*
Correct by }	*W. Petty*

I worked hard to bring it up to this, as I knew that I should not be able to go out with the case much after the chapel was opened.

Mr. Cennick in his affecting narrative of persecution in returning from the Baptist Chapel, Stratton, says,

"At last we came to a part of our road where were many gates, &c." It is worthy of remark that this is the very spot by which the chapel has been erected, as if God intended that it should be a monument to commemorate the triumph of his Gospel over cruel and brutish persecution.

Soon after the opening of the new chapel, a very interesting family, Mr. and Mrs. G. Pocock came to reside at Bourton some five miles off. They came over pretty regularly to worship with us at New Swindon, there being no place of worship in their village. This they found to be rather inconvenient and, more than that, they felt the moral destitution of the villagers who had no place of worship to go to, so that they wished to see them supplied with one. Mr. Pocock invited me to go and preach to the people in a small house which would be, for a little time, at my service. I went for some time on week evenings, and was much pleased with the numbers that attended, the attention paid, and the thankfulness of the hearers. Mr. Pocock observed one day that it was a pity that we had not a better place to meet in, and "as you are going to London," he said, "I wish you would call upon my landlord, H. Tucker Esq. and tell him the present state of things, and ask him to build us a small chapel. He is a very kind gentleman and may feel disposed to help us, and if not, I feel assured that he will not be offended with you for asking the favour at his hands."

To cut an interesting tale short, I went to London, called upon the gentleman and delivered my message. He made a few judicious enquiries and spoke several kind words, and above all he said he would take the matter into consideration. Well, thought I to myself, I have done a good day's work today. Some three months after this, Mrs. Tucker laid the foundation stone of the new chapel, a worthy lady who is always pleased to strengthen the hands and heart of her beloved husband in the performance of his numerous works of piety in which he is so abundantly engaged. The spacious sanctuary was at length finished and a very good house built for the officiating minister; no expense spared to make things comfortable; in every respect, I should say, worthy of the liberal donor. I went to the opening of the chapel, on which occasion the Hon. and Rev^d. Baptist Noel preached two truly excellent sermons. The gospel trumpet gave forth a very certain sound that day and the same glorious truths have been, I believe, faithfully announced there to this day, and much good has been done. It was said of the emperor Augustus that he found Rome built of brick, but that he left it built of marble. It may be truly said of this worthy gentleman, that he found Bourton a poor rustic hamlet, and he has made it already a model village. And that morally he found it destitute of the light of Truth, but that it is now blessed with something like the blissful dawn of the millennial day. It is also said, "The sun was risen upon the earth when Lot entered into Zoar."[4] Surely we have something like it in this case. May God raise up many such merchant princes to bless our English villages.

I preached at Upper Stratton, and had the superintendence of the little chapel there in conjunction with other chapels for about 30 years, and God did not allow his gospel to be preached there in vain. Many pleasing remembrances I could unfold concerning this village. The kind gentleman who did so much for Bourton came here also. He some few years ago purchased a property in this parish, and has already built a very commodious Baptist Chapel there, a spacious schoolroom and has also fitted up a house for the minister. The minister and teacher are principally supported by himself, whilst he and his beloved wife devote much of their time to visiting the stations and strengthening the hands of the worthy labourers. From my inmost heart, I say "God Almighty bless them and spare their lives for many years to come, and give them a place in Heaven at last."

I often think with pleasure of the first fruits of my ministry in the New Swindon Chapel. A female was converted under one my first sermons there. She became very anxious and earnest about the salvation of her soul, and at length she found peace and much happiness, and continued for some months in that pleasing state of mind, when, rather unexpectedly, she was taken ill. I went often to see her in her affliction, and found her generally happy and hopeful, and she, at last, departed this life rejoicing in Jesus Christ her Saviour. Many similar cases I might record, cases of the most interesting character, it does my heart good to think of them, and the thought of meeting them again in the happy world, as the fruit of my ministry, is truly delightful.

The case of a man of the name of Golding, a workman in the factory,

---

[4] Zoar was one of the five cities of the plain along with Sodom, Gomorrah, Admah and Zeboiim. God allowed Lot to flee from Sodom to Zoar before he destroyed Sodom and the other three cities with fire and brimstone. From Genesis 19:23. *[Harpers Bible Dictionary, 1985]*

was very affecting. He had been a very bad man, drunken, quarrelsome and very cruel to his wife. He came to hear me one Sabbath evening and the word of God was blessed to his conversion. It was indeed a conversion, one of the most marvellous I ever witnessed, so that all who knew him were surprised at the change. He became sober, chaste in his conversation, kind and loving to all, and especially to his wife and his children, as if to make amends for his past cruelty. He wished to be baptized without delay, but we put it off, whether right or wrong; of course we were cautious in receiving candidates for baptism; and he had been till very recently so bad, that we were almost unwilling to own him as a brother. In process of time, however, we came to the conclusion that the Spirit of God had wrought a great change in the man, and we agreed to receive him into Christian fellowship. He continued remarkably zealous and loving to all, so much so that I really had fears lest his zeal should be too hot to last. It was remarkable. I returned home one evening from a journey, when I was informed poor Golding was seriously hurt by the machinery, and that he lay at an inn just by in a dangerous state constantly calling out for Mr. Breeze. I went and found the dear man awfully mangled, and no one present could hope for his recovery. I found, on enquiry, that he had been engaged in cleaning the cogs on the nut of a fly wheel, and that a lad had put the strap on the drum as usual, not knowing that the poor fellow was there. He was instantly drawn in between the teeth, his right arm was broken in two or three places, and the flesh was torn quite away from his breast, so that the movement of the lungs could be seen when he was extricated from his dreadful position. It was indeed a sad and sickly sight. The medical gentlemen were preparing to amputate the broken arm, but I privately suggested to them the undesirableness of this, and said that as there was no hope of saving life, why put the man to greater torture. The reply they gave me was this, that there was no chance as it was, but there might be a faint hope by making that effort. I sat by his side whilst this terrible work was proceeding, constantly moistening the mouth of the dear sufferer with small quantities of brandy and water, and continued to direct his mind to the true source of consolation as well as I could. He bore his sufferings with amazing fortitude and even rejoiced in Christ his Saviour, and often said what a mercy it was that he had been brought to know the value of religion before this great trial came. I stayed with him the most of the night and came to him early the next morning, stayed till midday, and left him then in a very happy frame of mind. Soon after I reached home, word came to say that the dear man had departed this life conscious and triumphant. I felt more than satisfied with the medical gentlemen; they evidently manifested great skill and much sympathy. The remains were buried at Stratton next Saturday, when a large body of men from the factory attended, who pleased me exceedingly, by their humanity, tenderness and deep sympathy. I could many a touching tale unfold, but time would fail me to tell all, even the fiftieth part.

One day I stood in the street in front of the new chapel A respectable looking man passing by in a hurry asked,

"Please, Sir, is this the way to the station?"

"No, Sir," I replied, "that is the wrong road."

"O dear," said he, "I fear I shall be too late."

"Sir," I said, "I hope we shall not be too late at the last." These few words reached his heart, and were the means of his conversion. He sent to me afterwards more than once to say so and to thank me for speaking to him as I did.

I met a man in a neighbouring town one day recently, and he made himself known to me, saying that he had been a preacher of the gospel for many years and that he had no doubt but that many precious souls had been saved through his instrumentality,

"But, Sir," said he, "I owe all this under God to you. A sermon I heard you preach some 25 years ago was the means of my salvation. I have often wished to tell you so, Sir, it always does me good to see you." &c, &c, &c.

I can name this as a positive fact, (as far as we can judge from appearances), that I seldom travel by rail or otherwise within a moderate distance from home without meeting persons who have received benefit under my ministry.

Some years ago a respectable young man came to reside in this town. A pious female, now in heaven, invited him to attend my ministry; he came, received a blessing and soon became a member of the church. We perceived that the young man had abilities for the ministry and he was encouraged to exercise them. He did so and became a very useful preacher of the gospel. I introduced him to the Baptist College at Bristol. He passed through his studies with considerable credit, to the great satisfaction of the tutors, and his friends generally, and now occupies an important position as a minister of Jesus Christ in one of our most populous cities.

Rev. Richard Breeze in retirement at Eastbourne

15

A FEW TALES OF CRUEL DEEDS

THE UNBAPTIZED INVFANTS excluded from the covenant mercies of God and not allowed even to be laid in their humble resting place, till after the setting of the sun.

I love babies. I believe in infant salvation. I think it possible. I believe it certain.

> Bold Infidelity! turn pale and die
> Beneath this stone four infants' ashes lie
> Say! are they lost or saved?
> If Death's by sin, they sinned because they're here
> If Heaven's by works, in heaven they can't appear
> Ah! Reason, how depraved, revere the sacred pages.
> The knot's untied.
> They died for Adam sinned, they live for Jesus died.

Our Father in heaven loves babies. How feelingly he pleaded for them with the disobedient prophet!

"And should not I spare Nineveh, that great city, wherein are more than six score thousand persons that cannot discern between their right hand and their left."[1]

---

[1] Jonah denounced Nineveh at God's command and prophesied its destruction. The people repented and abandoned their wicked ways, so that God did not bring on the disaster he had threatened. Jonah was angry at this. The quotation is God's answer to Jonah's displeasure. *[Jonah 4:11, New English Bible]*

Jesus Christ loves babies.
See Israel's gentle Shepherd stands
With all engaging charms.
See how He takes the tender lambs
And folds them in his arms.

The royal Psalmist loved his dear, afflicted, and dying babe, and wept and prayed for its recovery, and when it died, feeling convinced of its happiness he consoled his own sorrowing spirit by this sweet thought.

"I shall go to him, but he shall not return to me."

The clergy of St. Mark's, New Swindon, will not give Christian burial to unbaptized infants nor even allow the little outcasts to be interred till after sunset. "Tell it not in Gath"[2]. This being the case, the distressed parents came to me time after time in their trouble, and I certainly did all I could to help them. Some of the little ones were buried in front of our new chapel, several were taken to our overfilled cemetery at Stratton, and some I followed to St. Mark's burial ground, placing them in their shaded little graves behind the church after sunset, as a stern rule to be observed at the funerals of these dear little condemned ones, by all and at all times.

One dear lad, a scholar in our Sunday School, worked in the factory and was much beloved by his shopmates and all who knew him. He was one day caught by the machinery and was torn to pieces. It was a painful and sad sight! Great sympathy was expressed and it was the full intention of the people generally to give an open expression of their sorrowful feelings by following the mangled remains of the dear little fellow to the silent tomb. One man in the town, finding out that the youth had not been christened, said that the funeral should not take place till after sunset. This in a measure altered the arrangements and fewer persons attended on this account.

An interesting youth, an unbaptized scholar in our Sunday School, said to his parents one Sabbath evening,

"I will repeat my hymn and then go to bed." He did so very nicely and

---

[2] When David heard the news of the death of Saul and Jonathan, he lamented, "Tell it not in Gath, proclaim it not in the streets of Ashkelon. . . Fallen, fallen are the men of war; and their armour left on the field" *[New English Bible, 1970, II Samuel 1:20]*

then retired. In the morning he got up at his usual time and went off to his work. He had to assist others to unload a truck of coals, but, being a little off his guard, he was struck by the engine buffer of a passing train and killed upon the spot, being thrown against a post fifteen feet off. It was the work of a moment, soon all was over. The parents felt this sudden shock exceedingly and invited me to the funeral wishing me to hold a religious service in the hour before we went to the grave. This was my usual custom on these mournful occasions and I found it very profitable, as it gave me an opportunity of doing much good. I went and found the house very full, great attention was paid during the service and, at the close, I said that, as I should not be permitted to speak at the grave, I should propose that all present would offer up silent prayer to God immediately upon the coffin being lowered down into the grave, on behalf of the parents and friends of the departed and all present, that He would in his mercy bless this sudden and loud call of his providence to all concerned and especially to the inhabitants of the town at large. It was done just as I requested in the most solemn way I ever witnessed. Nothing was heard but suppressed whispers, sobs, and sighs for full two minutes. I never saw anything so affecting and solemn in my life.

Who says that the Church is in danger? I say so, but not in danger from dissenters. I have known and loved them for above half a century. They will not pull one stone down, but would rather help the true-hearted to strengthen all that is good in the church. Nor from the evangelical clergy. They are the buttresses of the Episcopal Church, and if a true man of their stamp were placed in every pulpit throughout the land the church would grow stronger and be more prosperous than ever and the dissenters would rejoice in that success.

The great curse of the church is Ritualism, a subtle enemy in the camp, assuming various evil forms, and their name is legion. If there are a few among the clergy and the laity who try to do good there are hosts who are bent upon mischief, reminding us of the proverb, "Every wise woman buildeth her house, but the foolish plucketh it down with her hands." May God overrule these great evils for good, and soon bring about a glorious reformation that we may see it and rejoice together, then the above degrading scenes would continue to be for ever among the dark and wretched things of the past.

I held the pastorate of the Baptist Church at New Swindon for nearly 17 years[3] and perhaps upon the whole I can reckon them among the happiest years of my life.

One Sabbath evening, the chapel being very full as usual, together with the numerous gas burners, made the place very hot so that when I came out of the pulpit I was quite in a bath of perspiration. When I got to the front door, I found the night very dark and stormy; however, I set off, but found it a hard task to get home. I never remember such a stormy night. Two young men, local preachers among the Wesleyans of the town went out that evening to hold a service at a village a few miles off. They returned in such a sad plight that they took a severe cold from which they never recovered, so that the dear young men have long since been laid in early graves from the effect of that stormy night. The following Sabbath I felt cold shivers pass over me, and on Monday evening, while at a public meeting at the New Town, I was taken seriously ill and got home with great difficulty. The doctor was called in and pronounced it to be gastric fever of a very dangerous sort. For weeks my life was despaired of; the doctors held out no hopes of recovery. At length it settled in my right foot, and gangrene set in, the flesh parted from the bone right from the ankles over the upper part of the foot to the toes. The bones and the tendons were plainly visible, the latter have not acted, as three of the smaller toes fail to perform their office. In time the flesh came again and new skin grew over it, so that in seven or eight months I found myself at large again and was soon able, partially, to resume my beloved work. I never felt so thankful in my life. To the medical gentlemen for their skill and attention. To my beloved wife for her unwearied tenderness and good nursing. To my children and relatives for kind sympathies. the Church, the congregation and my neighbours very generally for their anxious enquiries, and the kind wishes they expressed. To my ministerial brethren who so kindly supplied the pulpit during the months of my affliction, and to my people who gave

---

[3] '20' according to pencilled note which refers to the letter of invitation.

liberal collections to meet the travelling expenses of the good and efficient supplies who came to my help. Above all thanks to the Father of mercies; it is He who spared my life, raised me up again and has added to the number of my days, blessed be His Holy Name.

I resigned the pastoral charge of the Baptist Church, Swindon New Town, Feb 7, 1865, one of the most painful acts I ever did. The people had been very kind to me with an exception or two; I had built a chapel and saw it paid for; collected a church of upwards of 60 communicants, and that number would have been perhaps as large again but for the fluctuating character of the floating population of the place. There was scarcely a let-able sitting in the chapel, but what was occupied, and a flourishing Sunday School of some 300 children and teachers. and all this was brought about originally by God's blessing on my individual efforts and personal respon-sibility. The Rev^d. E. Matthews supplied the pulpit a few Sabbaths after I resigned. He called upon me to express his kind sympathy with me in my weakness and said that he had seen many congregations, both in America and in England, but few had pleased him so much as the one I had recently resigned. A gentleman called upon me a few months ago and said that he had often thought with pleasure of my well filled chapel, since the time he preached for me when he visited the place. Well, generally the congrega-tions were good and remarkably attentive. Few ministers ever preached to a kinder people than I had there. Exceptions there are doubtless in most congregations, but such are generally men of little minds and shallow piety, too contemptible to be noticed. Exceptions are not the general rule.

When the chapel was being erected, a gentleman said to me that he did not envy my undertaking; that I should have a horribly rough lot to deal with. Now I have found the people quite the reverse of this. They have al-ways treated me with the greatest respect. I have preached many times in the public streets, in the chapels, and have taken part in public meetings &c, but they have invariably treated me with the highest respect.

When it was reported at the time of my illness, that I was dead, there was a deep sympathy expressed by all the people of the town, and it was observed that many of the children wept when they heard the tidings. The report went through the whole factory rapidly, and in some cases the machinery was stopped for a short time when the men met in groups to express their sorrow at my supposed departure. This information I have received from the best authority, but I can easily believe it as I have never been treated with anything but respect and kindness by all the inhabitants of New Swindon among whom I have sojourned for 18 years of my life. That God may bless them and all their little ones and prepare me and them to meet in the happy world at last is the sincere prayer of my heart. Some time after I had resigned my charge, I received a purse containing sixty sovereigns as a kind memorial from the church and congregations and also from some personal friends and relatives who had heard of the circumstance. I considered this testimonial as a kind of acknowledgement of my hard labours and great pecuniary sacrifices in founding the above promising Interest in New Swindon; and most likely it was intended as such by the liberal donors themselves. I feel it, and have felt it, for nearly 50 years a great honour to labour and make sacrifices to promote the cause of Jesus Christ in any way I can, but, at the same time I could not recommend a brother minister to do as I have done unless he has personal property at command, and a single eye to the glory of God in what he does. Still, after all our doings to aid the good cause, we shall have our dying regrets when we depart this life. We shall indeed feel sorry that we have not loved Jesus Christ more and served him more faithfully.

God having saved me from the love and power of sin for nearly 50 years, I feel very confident that he will also save me from the penalty of sin in the life to come. When I was about making a profession of Religion, my earnest prayer was that God would never allow me to dishonour it, and to his goodness and faithfulness I record it that hitherto the Lord hath helped me. Through all the changes of my long pilgrimage, my outward conduct may be said to have been blameless and my Christian reputation unspotted. I take no credit of this to myself. I give all the praise to God from whom all good proceeds. Blessed be His Holy Name.

His love in time past forbids me to think
He'll leave me at last in trouble to sink,
Each sweet Ebenezer I have in review
Confirms his good pleasure to help me quite through.

After I had closed my labours at the New Town, and had been favoured with comparative ease for a few weeks, although my strength was weakness, I could not feel comfortable. It seemed as if the world had ceased to go its rounds, as if the church had ceased to work, and the great enemy had all his own way, and I looked on and did nothing to remedy this state of things. I felt sad, very unhappy, indeed nothing like it can I remember in all my experience. It may have been the force of habit! I had been in harness for nearly half a century, always hard on, both mind and body engaged in incessant conflict, and to sit down in inglorious ease was more than I could do with anything like cheerfulness. When in this state of mind, I received a letter from the good people attending the Baptist Chapel at Kingston Lisle, inviting me to preach to them on the following Lord's Day, as my good friend and brother the Rev^d. Robt Aikenhead of Wantage had informed them that I had resigned my charge at Swindon. I went there and preached to the good people on the Sabbath day and on the following Friday received an unanimous and loving invitation to settle over them as their pastor. Their late pastor was the Rev^d. Robt Townsend, a student from the Baptist College, Bristol, a truly good and excellent man, a scholar, a gentleman and a Christian. Being a man of very retired habits he continued in that secluded locality for about 36 years to minister to the few people who attended and to superintend a small endowed school in connection with their place of worship. His respectable abilities would have commanded a very different position, but it appears that the dear man preferred the quiet village to the crowded town. He departed this life in the full assurance of faith to the regret of many and especially of the poor people in the neighbourhood in the week that closed my work at Swindon.

I accepted the kind invitation on condition that I might engage the help of my old friend and successor at Lechlade, Mr. Walsh, to take to the school, and to assist me in the work of the ministry for which he was very competent. These matters having been amicably arranged, we entered upon the good work and have continued it to this day and, through mercy, not without pleasing tokens of the Divine presence and blessing.

It might gratify the historian and the antiquarian if I were to write a chapter about this rural village and the numerous relics of antiquity found in the neighbourhood.

We have near us the celebrated Ashdown Hill, and a fine open hilly country where many a fearful battle has been fought in days gone by; Lord Craven's beautiful mansion and park, the White House of great celebrity; the White Horse Hill, where king Alfred fought his first battle with the Danes and won it. Then we have the renowned spot called Dragon Hill, where it is said George killed the dragon, thrusting his keen lance into the reptile's heart with such deadly force, that it caused the blood to gush out with such intense heat that it destroyed the grass, roots and all, and that the spot on which it fell has continued bare to the present day. Then we have a little over the hill towards the South, Wayland Smith's Cave, an underground dwelling place where lived a blacksmith, cattle doctor, &c, who could make himself invisible, and do many marvellous things too numerous to mention. Should the reader curiously wish to know more about these marvellous localities, let him consult Sir Walter Scott's *Kenilworth* and there he will find all he wants upon the subject. If that will not satisfy him, let him read *The Scouring of the White Horse* by the author of *Tom Brown's School Days*. Adjoining the village of Kingston Lisle we have the lovely park and beautiful mansion of [E. M.] Atkins Esq. Few country gentlemen can boast of a home more lovely than his. May he and his beloved lady and young family live many happy years to adorn the time-honoured name which they bear. Who has not heard of Kingston Lisle's "Blowing Stone" and its marvellous powers. For a description of this stone and all other unusual curiosities in this locality, I must refer to the above able and popular authors.

I feel thankful that I am able now in my 71st year to supply the chapels of Kingston Lisle and Stratton St. Margaret on alternate Sabbaths with so few failures. Still, I find my physical powers waning and my mental capabilities not equal to what they once were. I feel daily that I am nearing that bourne from whence no traveller returns, but I fear no evil, why should I? God is my Father, Jesus Christ is my Saviour and the Holy Spirit is my Sanctifier, the triune Jehovah is my eternal refuge, my hope rests upon the blood of Christ.

> Other refuge have I none
> Hangs my helpless soul on thee.

When the time comes when the grand secret shall be revealed, I believe the verdict will be in my favour. "Saved by faith in Christ." Should I after all be out in my calculation, it will be to me an awful disappointment, which will be, I believe, an utter impossibility. I often think of the beloved relatives and Christian friends who have gone to the heavenly world and of my own dear children, who are gone to the happy state of the blessed. Of their present glory, I have not the shadow of a doubt.

The Lord blessed me and my beloved wife with six children. It has pleased him to take three of them to himself. These three are now members of the church triumphant above, and as the three that God has kindly spared to us, are members of the church militant, we fondly hope that we are all saved with an everlasting salvation. There are many families in heaven of which not one member is missing and I do hope, and pray every day, that we as a family may all be found there to meet to part no more for ever.

The first child we were called upon to give up was an infant, eleven weeks old. The names we had given him were Samuel Pearce Breeze. The little one died at Downington House and was buried on the south side of Mr. and Mrs. Loys' tomb, in front of the Baptist Chapel, Lechlade. The second was our dearly loved daughter Sarah Susannah Breeze.[44] She died at the Chapel House, New Swindon and was interred in front of the new

---

[4] Samuel Pearce Breeze died, 22 January, 1838, of inflammation, Lechlade, aged 11 weeks. *[Certificate #61, 1/4 1838, Reg District Faringdon, Sub-district Faringdon, Berks, Oxford and Gloucester]* ; Sarah Susannah Breeze died on 12 September, 1849, at New Swindon, aged 13 years and 9 months, daughter of Richard Breeze, Dissenting Minister, of phthisis pulmonalis (certified) Richard Breeze present at the death. *[Certificate number 123, Registration district of Swindon, County of Wilts., third quarter of 1849]*

Chapel. She was less than 14 years old, nearly grown to womanhood, very clever, very aimiable, and truly lovely in her deportment, and, above all, a true and intelligent Christian. She was very patient and resigned to the will of God during her long affliction, and when the hour of release came she met the great enemy with amazing calmness and fortitude. It was an affecting scene. While she was struggling with death, we all knelt at her bedside in earnest and confiding prayer to our dear Saviour that he would receive her spirit into his kind arms, to dwell in his presence for ever. I believe that she had been a real Christian from her infancy, as she said, some time before her departure, that she did not know a time when she did not love Jesus Christ, but that she knew she loved him sincerely from the fifth year of her age. The third was my dear firstborn, William Beckingsale Breeze.[5] He was nearly 21 years of age when he departed this life. He died in the same room as his sister in the presence of his weeping parents, his only brother, and two sisters, and was buried by the grave of his beloved sister Sarah, who had preceded him to the heavenly rest only about two years.

These were great trials to us all, yet they were productive of good. They have led us to think more of Heaven than we ever did before, it feels more like a sweet home, having part of the dear family gone there already and we are hastening onwards to rejoin them in our Father's house above. There is one other great good I have most assuredly derived from these afflictive dispensations; I do not fear death so much as I did.

God having helped my dear children to triumph over him so valiantly, I feel assured that my Saviour, in whom alone I trust will help me in that terrible conflict as he helped them, and untold millions besides.

> Thou are gone to the grave, but we will not deplore thee
> Whose God is thy ransom, thy guardian and guide;
> He gave thee, He took thee, and He will restore thee,
> And Death hath no sting for the Saviour hath died!

---

5 William Beckingsale Breeze died on 29 July 1852 in New Town, Swindon, aged 21 years, chemist and druggist. Cause of death, scrofala [sic], disease of mesenteric gland (certified. Richard Breeze present at the death. *[Certificate no. 228, third quarter of 1852, Registrar's district of Swindon, County of Wilts.]*

Grave the guardian of thy dust
Grave the treasure of the skies
Every atom of thy truth
Rests in hope again to rise.

Appendix I

The Romans in Gloucestershire

*An able and interesting lecture delivered at Gloucester, 1860
by the Reverend Samuel Lysons, M.A. Abridged, with
additions from other authors by Richard Breeze.*

The first attempt at invasion upon England, by the Romans was made in the year 54 B.C. by the Emperor Julius Caesar. He does not appear, however, to have made any settlement in the Island, or to have gained much advantage, beyond making it known to his own countrymen. Julius Caesar made two different descents upon England. In each case his fleet seemed to have suffered considerably from storms, while his army met with a very stubborn resistance from our British ancestors; so that Lucan, Eutropius, Tacitus, Dion and Quintilian unite, in shearing him of the credit which he gives himself for success, and say that he was glad enough to get away safe and sound.

The next invasion of our country was made by Aulus Plautius, a general of the Emperor Claudius; for though Caligula intended it, he was satisfied to stand upon the heights of the opposite shore, look across the straits of Dover, and then go home again.

The arrival of Plautius was, as we learn from Dion Cassius, in the year A.D. 45, and then the county of Gloucester was first brought in contact with the Romans, for the Britons not expecting this sudden invasion, fled in dismay, whereupon the Roman general pursued them into the interior of the country and compelled the Cobuni, or inhabitants of Gloucestershire under Caractacus, their king, first to submit to the impetuosity of his arms.

The first surprise being over, our Gloucestershire predecessors were not at all inclined to let the invader have his own way, and they offered them the most spirited resistance. After several battles with varied success, in which the Roman general found them very courageous and resolute, Aulus Plautius wrote home to the Emperor, saying that he had better come and bring reinforcements with him if he had hopes of keeping the country; upon which Claudius fitted out a very powerful army, put himself at the head, and advanced against the Britons. Claudius landed somewhere on the south east coast and, following the course of the Thames up to its source, near Cirencester, made his way over the Cotteswold [*sic*] Hills towards the Vale of Gloucester, to which his general, Aulus Plautius, had already penetrated.

Arviragus, the then ruler of this country (Caractacus having been taken prisoner), was only too glad to come to a compromise with the Emperor by accepting his daughter Genissa, or Gewise, in marriage; a politic measure on the part of the Emperor, who thereby expected to graft Roman civilization upon the barbarous manners of the Dobunian king.

All authors agree that Claudius' government of this country was tempered with mildness and great moderation, which had a happy effect upon the natives.

In taking possession of one of their chief places, called in their language Cair Ghow, or the fair city, latinized into the name of *Glevum*, Claudius established a Roman colony there which was called Claudiocestria in his honour. The discovery of the coins of Claudius, as having taken place at Kingsholm, close adjoining the city of Gloucester, indicate the place as being the site of a royal residence, as King's Holm, or Ham, means a house or home, thus King's Ham is the king's palace. Gloucester was, in short, a most important city, and governed by officers of the highest rank in the Imperial Government. Aulus Plautius was a man of consular rank; and we read of Gloucester sending a consul, as ambassador, to grace King Arthur's court on the occasion of his coronation.

The stay of the Emperor appears to be short and on his departure he left his favourite general, Aulus Plautius, in charge of the newly acquired territory, as *propraetor*, or governor-general, and perhaps as guardian and protector to his daughter, so recently married to this barbarian chief. And here comes a most interesting incident in the history of this town. Aulus Plautius' wife, Pomponia Graecina by name, says Tacitus, was a Christian, the first in Britain, says Tindal.

Whether he had authority for stating so much it is hard to say, as some writers give that honour to Simon, the Canaanite, others to Joseph of Arimethea.

We have, nevertheless, this interesting fact that the Christian religion was professed by Pomponia Claudia, &c, in Gloucester, in 45 A.D. or only eleven years after our Saviour's crucifixion.

We soon find the latter lady brought into connexion with Claudia Ruffina, a noble British lady, professing the same faith; though whether Claudia was converted by Pomponia or Pomponia by Claudia, we have no direct evidence, but that they resided at Gloucester together at a very early date appears very certain. Speed and Jones positively assert that Rome derives its Christianity from Britain and not Britain from Rome. There were Christians in Rome before either Paul or Peter visited that city. This we have every reason to believe, that "the saints that are in Caesar's household", mentioned by St. Paul,[1] as then congregated at Rome, *viz* Claudia and Pudens, called Rufus, and many of Caesar's household. Claudia was celebrated for her learning and beauty.

> From painted Britons, how was Claudia born
> The fair barbarian, how do arts adorn?
> When Roman charmed a Grecian soul commend
> Athens and Rome may well for her contend.
>
> Martial

Thus Martial speaks of Claudia in his Epigrams, and we may add that Gloucestershire may well be proud of her also.

But it may be asked how I connect Claudia with Gloucestershire and with the Dobuni? I answer that [it] is from her connexion with Pomponia, the wife of Aulus Plautius, who resided at Gloucester as vice-emperor and Chief of the *Legio Claudiocestriae.*

Jones, of Oswestry, considers that her name Ruffina was her own British name of Griffin, of Griffith, latinized by a Roman termination, and that

---

[1] From Philippians 4, 22: "Give my greetings, in the fellowship of Christ Jesus, to each one of God's people. The brothers who are now with me send their greetings to you, and so do all God's people here, particularly those who belong to the imperial establishment." *[New English Bible]*

she probably took the name of Claudia out of compliment to the Emperor Claudius with the members of whose court she resided. She must have been a sister of the British King, Arviragus, whom, Jones, the learned Welsh scholar, makes identical with Lucius. He says his British name was Lluys (?) Coel-ap-Meirig, or Meyrick; the name of Arviragus, Ap-Viragus, as he is indiscriminately called, is readily deduced from Ap-Meirig.

Pudens, the husband whom Claudia married, was most likely converted by her, as we know from an inscription on a stone found in Chichester about 1730 that he was a pagan when he came into Britain.

Speed, quoting Bale, says that Pudens Rufus was a "Roman gentleman, a colonel, afterwards a senator, a man of mild disposition, naturally modest, a great philosopher of the sect of the Stoics." But to connect our Rufus entirely with this city, a tomb-stone bearing the name of Rufus was discovered in a field near the old London Road in 1826 or 1827 (the ancient Ermine Street), and may be seen at the present day. It contains a Latin inscription and is thus translated, or may be so:

> "Rufus, a Commissary-General, of the Equestrian Order and Officer of Cavalry, commanding the Sixth Legion, having served eleven years in the Thacian Regiment of Cavalry, and twenty-two years in the Army, is buried here. This monument his heirs have carefully erected, to the terms of his will."

It is said that Claudia built the first Christian church at Rome and dedicated it to St. Peter and St. Paul, and we read of her at Rome as instrumental in converting many to her faith in the time of Nerva. Some assert that, at her request, Paul came over to Britain, and, as there is a period of nine years, or eleven, unaccounted for in the history of Paul, *viz*, from his first imprisonment [in] A.D. 50, to his martyrdom at Rome in A.D. 69, [this] rendered the supposition probable.

It is certain that this apostle, in the eight years between his first imprisonment in Rome and his return to Jerusalem, propagated the Christian religion in several places, especially in the western countries.

Now, the likeliest times for the conversion of the Britons was between the victory of Claudius and the defeat of Boadicea; for at the period of this general revolt there were in the island above 80,000 Romans, among whom were very many Christians.

Tacitus speaks of the opulence and splendour of Prasaturgus, King of the British Iceni, husband of Boadicea, whose dress is described of exceeding richness, with ample folds and plaits, and also her chain of gold is described as rich and valuable, and her eloquence is said to have been a model for Caesar himself. We know they had the means of coining money, for the coins of Cassibelan, Cunobelin, Arviragus, and Boadicea are in the collections of antiquaries. They had ships with which they traded to the neighbouring coasts and, had they been such utter barbarians as often described by historians, is it likely that the kind-hearted Emperor Claudius would have married his daughter to one of their kings?

Only imagine our good King George the Third having married one of his daughters to an Ojibbeway [sic] a Cherokee, or a Creek Indian Chief; or our present beloved Sovereign handing over one of her charming princesses to Rupparah, or Rangeheita, or any other Maoree [sic] chief in New Zealand!

I confess that I have a strong inclination myself to believe in the tradition of our Asiatic origin, though it would be impossible to assign a positive date to the colonization of this country. And whether our ancestors came from Troy, Carthage, with Brutus, the son of Æneas, as the tradition is, I am not prepared to say, yet I am not inclined to treat all these traditions as fabulous, or to throw over all our early history [as?] John Milton, in his *History of England*, 8 vol, 1677, p. 11. The same writer also says that the language the Britons used when Julius Caesar came here was a kind of Greek. Had there been no affinity between the languages how was it that the eloquence of Caracticus was so readily recognized when carried prisoner to Rome, direct from Britain?

Gray says, if there be anything at all in a common root of a language, or similarity of names, there is a strong evidence of our Phoenician descent, to say nothing of a similarity of worship, which is not unimportant. The temples of all these kindred nations were circular in their form, like Stonehenge, symbolical of the sun, which they worshipped, and the temple of Avebury, Wiltshire, bears also a circular character, by its circle with circle, considered by many antiquaries to represent an immense serpent or dragon.

In the destruction of the Pythian serpent, or dragon, by Apollo, one can scarcely fail to detect the tradition of the destruction of him who was emphatically called "the old serpent" by that holy one who was to be called, "the Sun of Righteousness" (Fuller's Ch[urch] History)

Immediately on Claudius' gaining a footing in this country, he set about the formation of grand military roads for the purpose of conveying his troops and baggage, and he built a chain of fortresses along the line of the brow of the Cotteswold Hills, overhanging the Vale of Severn. These forts were designed to act as a check upon the Silures whose country extended from the other side [of] the Severn, westward beyond the Forest of Dean &c. (Tacitus)

The Severn was the boundary between the Dobunes and the Silures as also between the two great divisions which the Romans afterwards made on the southern parts of Britain, into Britannia Prima and Britannia Secunda, including the territories above named.

The Roman roads were supposed to have been British roads originally and only adopted, improved and extended by the Romans.

Higden attributes the *quatuor Viai Militares* [sic] to Belinus, the British King, *viz*; the Foss, from south to north, through Bath, Cirencester and Cotteswold to Scotland; the Watling Street, from Dover to Wales; the Beling Street, from St. David's to Southampton; and the Ichneild Street from St. David's to Tynemouth, Northumberland. The Ichneild Street, or *Via Icenica*, led from the Iceni, who inhabited the present county of Norfolk, to Wales, entering Gloucestershire near Eastleach, passing through Cirencester (Cainum, Cirinum?), one of the earliest Roman towns in this county and the capital of the Cotteswolds, and crossed the Severn at Aust, to Isca on Caerleon in Monmouthshire. Several others may be named such as the *Via Salaria*, or Salt Way, as the road which enters the county near Lechlade, passes through the parishes of Quenington, Coln St. Aldwin's, Coln St. Denis, crosses the Foss Road between Northleach and Foss Bridges and proceeds probably to Gloucester, &c.

These roads were lined by houses or Roman villas, some three miles apart or so, and are often discovered to this day. The roads are called streets in British, Ystraed, and in Latin, *strata*, from the roads being pitched or paved with stone.

We have it from good authority that the Romans founded 20 cities in Britain, the power they swayed and the influence they could exert must have been immense. I need not say that God used that power and that influence in a remarkable manner, to spread his gospel among the people.

The Roman authorities were not favourable to Christianity, it is true; in general they thought it a harmless superstition and troubled themselves but little about it, still the gospel had warm-hearted and influential friends at Court, and many true and zealous Christians in the armies too.

At Court there were the Arviragus, (or Lucius), the first Christian King in Britain and his queen Genessa; the Emperor's daughter, Pomponia, the pious wife of Aulus Plautius, the Governor-General; and the zealous and lovely Claudia, the British princess, and her Christian husband, Pudens Rufus, Commissary General, &c. The combined and untiring efforts of these warm-hearted Christians must have been very great, and their success must have been unprecedented.

Tertullian, Origen, Bede and Gildas, all bear testimony to the progress Christianity had made in Britain during the first two centuries, even in places inaccessible to the Roman Army, as well as Roman territory, which is confirmed by the multitude of British martyrs who suffered in the cruel persecutions of Diocletian and Maximinian.

In the reign of Constantine, Christian churches abounded in Britain and, in 596, Augustine came with 40 monks to convert England to the Christian truth by his inhuman massacre of the British clergy of Bangor.

That Christianity was firmly established in this country, even though bitterly persecuted by the Saxons, is proved by the fact that Augustine caused to be put to death no less than 1250 of British clergy because they would not submit to the See of Rome. (Jones of Oswestry)

APPENDIX II

Unanimous expression of regret from the association at Fairford on Richard Breeze's decision to leave Lechlade

Chipping Norton. June 19th, 1847

My Dear Sir,

I have the pleasure to forward to you the accompanying resolution which was unanimously agreed to at the closing meeting of the association at Fairford. Cordially assenting to its expressions of respect and sympathy.

I am, dear Sir,

Very truly yours,

Thos. Bliss

Revd R. Breeze. Lechlade

(Copy)

Memo: Made at a meeting of ministers at the close of the Association.

Fairford, 3rd June, 1847

The brethren have learned with sincere regret that our respected R. Breeze is about to leave Lechlade, the scene of his long continued and honourable services in the cause of Christ.

They fear that his active and discursive labours in the ministry will cause that his loss will be long felt by the good people in that neighbourhood, and by the entire of this association which has so often been cheered by the presence and the reports of our esteemed brother at its meetings. But, not questioning the correctness of his views in effecting this removal, we heartily commend our brother to the blessing of Heaven, and the esteem of all good men.

Signed by order of} Thos. Bliss, B.A.

the meeting} Moderator

APPENDIX III

The church being formed, I received from its members the following unanimous invitation

Swindon, Aug. 13, 1855

To the Revd R. Breeze,

Dear Sir,

We, whose names are undersigned, being members and communicants of the Baptist church at the Swindon New Town, having unanimously passed a resolution at a church meeting on the Sabbath evening of July 29th 1855, to the effect that you continue in the pastoral office of the Church, but hearing that it has since been stated that we did not mean what we then so unitedly expressed, think it desirable to be more explicit.

We do therefore, after deliberate thought and prayer to God for direction in this matter, affix our names to this document to express in writing the hopes that you will accede to our wishes by continuing the pastoral office among us, as you have hitherto done with so much honour and effect.

That God may more abundantly bless your endeavours to promote his cause among us, our beloved families and the thousands of immortal beings residing in this locality, is the sincere and earnest prayer of, Dear Sir, yours very affectionately in the bonds of the Gospel of our Lord and Saviour, Jesus Christ.

INDEX